£10

The Great Fami

Maynooth Studies in Local History

SERIES EDITOR Raymond Gillespie

This volume is one of six short books published in the Maynooth Studies in Local History series in 2018. Like their predecessors they range widely, both chronologically and geographically, over the local experience in the Irish past. Chronologically they span the worlds of medieval Tristernagh in Westmeath, a study of an early 19th-century land improver, the Famine of the 1840s in Kinsale, politics and emigration in the late 19th century and sectarian rituals in the late 19th and 20th centuries. Geographically they range across the length of the country from Derry to Kinsale and westwards from Westmeath to Galway. Socially they move from those living on the margins of society in Kinsale and Galway in the middle of the 19th century to the politics and economics of the middle class revealed in the world of Thomas Bermingham and the splits in Westmeath in the 1890s. In doing so they reveal diverse and complicated societies that created the local past, and present the range of possibilities open to anyone interested in studying that past. Those possibilities involve the dissection of the local experience in the complex and contested social worlds of which it is part as people strove to preserve and enhance their positions within their local societies. Such studies of local worlds over such long periods are vital for the future since they not only stretch the historical imagination but provide a longer perspective on the shaping of society in Ireland, helping us to understand the complex evolution of the Irish experience. These works do not simply chronicle events relating to an area within administrative or geographically determined boundaries, but open the possibility of understanding how and why particular regions had their own personality in the past. Such an exercise is clearly one of the most exciting challenges for the future and demonstrates the vitality of the study of local history in Ireland.

Like their predecessors, these six short books are reconstructions of the socially diverse worlds of the poor as well as the rich, women as well as men, the geographical marginal as well as those located near the centre of power. They reconstruct the way in which those who inhabited those worlds lived their daily lives, often little affected by the large themes that dominate the writing of national history. They also provide models that others can follow up and adapt in their own studies of the Irish past. In such ways will we understand better the regional diversity of Ireland and the social and cultural basis for that diversity. They, with their predecessors, convey the vibrancy and excitement of the world of Irish local history today.

Maynooth Studies in Local History: Number 134

The Great Famine in Kinsale

Catherine Flanagan

FOUR COURTS PRESS

Set in 10pt on 12pt Bembo by
Carrigboy Typesetting Services for
FOUR COURTS PRESS LTD
7 Malpas Street, Dublin 8, Ireland
www.fourcourtspress.ie
and in North America for
FOUR COURTS PRESS
c/o IPG, 814 N Franklin St, Chicago, IL 60622

© Catherine Flanagan and Four Courts Press 2018

ISBN 978–1–84682–723–5

All rights reserved. Without limiting the rights under
copyright reserved alone, no part of this publication may
be reproduced, stored in or introduced into a retrieval system,
or transmitted, in any form or by any means (electronic,
mechanical, photocopying, recording or otherwise), without
the prior written permission of both the copyright
owner and the above publisher of this book.

Printed in Ireland
by SprintPrint, Dublin.

Contents

Acknowledgments	6
Introduction	7
1 Pre-Famine Kinsale	11
2 Famine, death and disease in Kinsale Union	22
3 Kinsale workhouse	51
Conclusion	64
Appendices	66
Notes	70

FIGURES

1	Map of Kinsale in 1838	8
2	Local variations in housing, 1841	13
3	Yearly admissions to Kinsale workhouse, 1842–5	20
4	Proportion of inmates across electoral divisions, 1842–5	21
5	Total number of inmates in Kinsale workhouse (1847–51) versus capacity (1847–9)	57
6	Number of deaths recorded in Kinsale workhouse, 1848–9	58

TABLES

1	Statistics for housing in the barony of Kinsale, 1841: number and proportion of families in each class of house, in Kinsale town and rural areas of barony	13
2	Kinsale union relief committees: subscriptions collected locally and government donations received, 1846	27
3	Number of admissions to Kinsale workhouse and number and percentage of deaths recorded from October 1846 to July 1847	45
4	Record of deaths in Kinsale workhouse from January 1846 to December 1852	47
5	Workhouse weekly orders and cost of a pauper from 1846 to 1850	54

Acknowledgments

My sincere thanks to the Department of History, University College Cork, and in particular my supervisor, Dr Larry Geary, for affording me the opportunity to complete a thesis on the Great Famine in Kinsale on which this book is based. I am deeply indebted to Dr Geary for his encouragement and advice on my thesis and for initially introducing me to this most painful period in Irish history with his enlightening lecture series, 'The People's Health'. I am especially grateful to Professor Raymond Gillespie, series editor, Maynooth Studies in Local History, who accepted this study for publication. I would like to acknowledge the generous help and cooperation of the staff of the following: UCC library, especially Special Collections, Cork City and County Archives, Cork County Library, Skibbereen and Kinsale branches, National Archives of Ireland, National Library of Ireland and the Sisters of Mercy, Kinsale. I wish to extend a special thanks to Sr Joan who allowed me access to the unpublished annals in Kinsale convent. Members of Kinsale Historical Society, especially Gerry McCarthy, have encouraged and supported me in my endeavours and I am very grateful for their help. I wish to thank Carol and Sarah O'Brien for the cover sketch of Kinsale workhouse and to my family and friends for their unending support and encouragement. Finally, I deeply appreciate the help and advice of my husband, Ray, in bringing this study to fruition.

Introduction

The Great Famine of 1845–52 marked a watershed in Irish history. At least one million people died from dearth or famine-related diseases and over a million emigrated, changing the demographics of the country forever. The scale of the Great Famine was cataclysmic, with the poor suffering the most as an entire social class – cottiers, beggars, vagrants and labourers – was destroyed. The potato was the staple diet for over half of the population and the appearance of potato blight, *phytophthora infestans*, in the second week of September 1845 signalled the greatest calamity ever to beset Ireland.

The scale and severity of the Great Famine varied regionally and even locally across the country. In some areas, such as Skibbereen, the Great Famine is well documented. In other areas, like Kinsale, there is a dearth of research and publications on the subject. Skibbereen is strongly identified with the Famine and was one of the worst affected areas in the country. In the early years of the Famine, the appalling level of distress was highlighted by travellers to the town and as a result Skibbereen received infamy in the press. After the sesquicentenary commemoration in the mid-1990s, local historians published numerous books and articles on the Famine in west Cork. The Skibbereen Famine Commemoration Committee compiled two volumes of *Sources for the history of the Great Famine in Skibbereen and surrounding areas*. The purpose of these volumes was to make local historical source material on the Famine accessible.

One of the contributors to these volumes, Peter Foynes, subsequently published *The Great Famine in Skibbereen*, which describes the events in Skibbereen and district during the worst years of the calamity. Foynes' assessment of the pre-Famine era is largely positive. Although the area was poor and densely populated with the potato central to the economy and to the sustenance of the majority of the people, he cites the presence of an agricultural show as an indication of the general air of improvement in the region. After the onset of blight, Foynes is critical of the relief measures instigated by the government as they failed to understand the pivotal role of the 'humble' potato. He argues that the relief measures from the outset (importation of Indian corn and public works) only worked due to the partial failure of the potato crop in 1845 and subsequently the public works failed as low, task-work wages could not possibly sustain a debilitated workforce in a free market economy. The Famine hit Skibbereen earlier and harder than in other parts of the county. For the winter of 1846–7, Foynes covers in detail the poverty, suffering, disease, death, emigration and the responses from the government to the crisis. He describes the social conditions in Skibbereen from the inquests held into the deaths of men on public works in October 1846. By 1848, the worst of the crisis was over

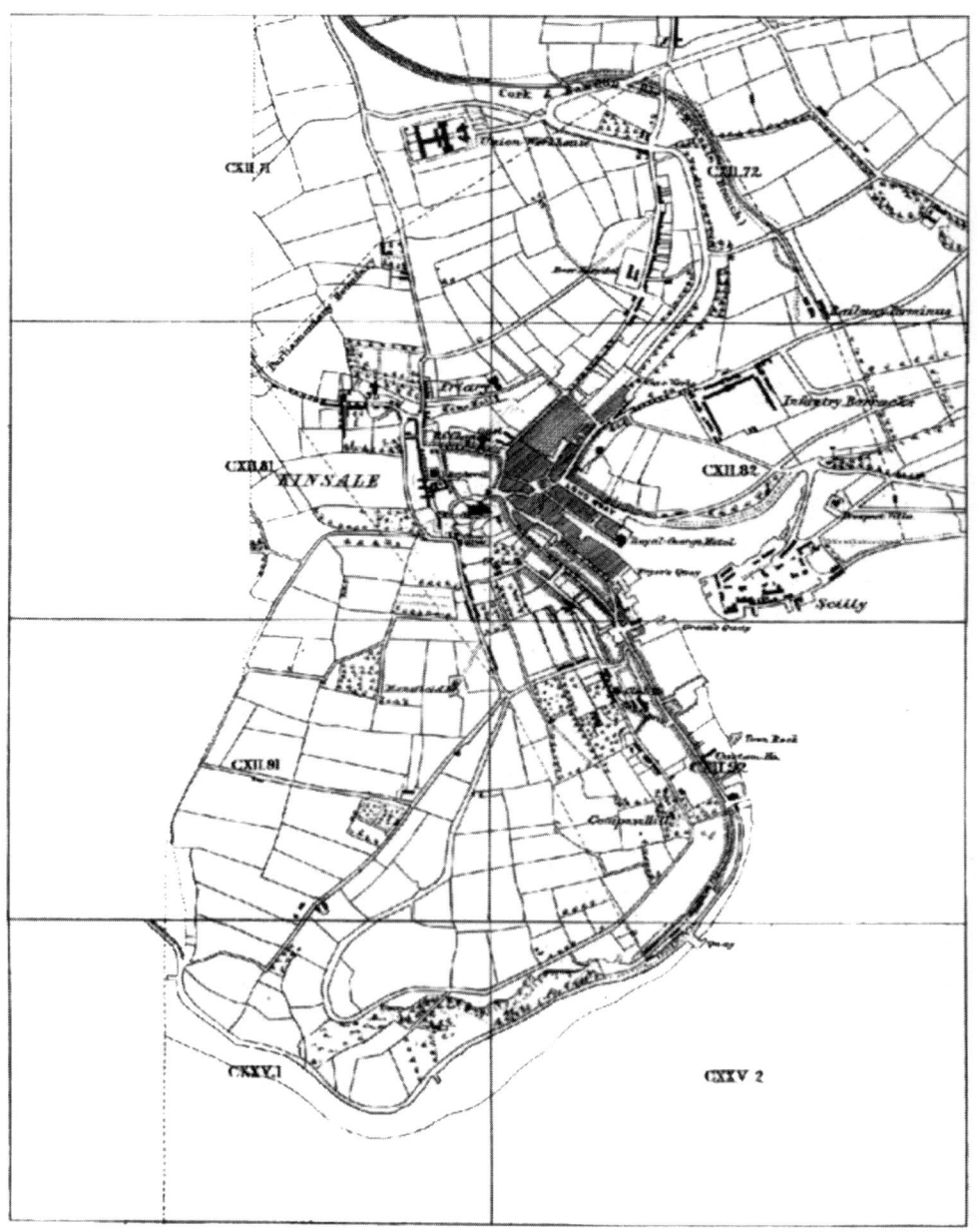

1. Map of Kinsale in 1838

Source: Ordnance Survey Index to the Map of the Town of Kinsale held by Ordnance Survey Ireland. © Public domain. Scale: Six inches to one statue mile.

in Skibbereen. Foynes concludes that the social upheaval and population decline was not much different to other parts of the country but what distinguishes Skibbereen was the magnitude of the calamity that created them.

The most definitive account of the Famine in west Cork is undoubtedly Patrick Hickey's book – *Famine in West Cork: the Mizen Peninsula: land and people, 1800–1852*. Hickey examines the economic, social, religious and political conditions in the pre-Famine era. He concurs with Foynes' assessment that there was a general air of improvement with considerable progress made from 1823 to 1845. Hickey provides a detailed narrative of the famine in the Mizen Peninsula and some neighbouring parishes. His chapter on mortality and emigration (1846–7) is particularly enlightening as he presents data for six parishes – Kilmoe, Schull/Ballydehob, Kilcoe, Caheragh, Drimoleague and Drinagh. A return of deaths and emigration for the six parishes compiled by J.J. Marshall, poor law inspector for Skibbereen union, gives an insight into the harrowing suffering endured by the people. Hickey presents this data in tabular and graphic form, which shows that the western parishes suffered the highest mortality. The intensity of the famine in Schull was equal to Skibbereen and earned both places lasting notoriety as the 'famine-slain sisters of the south'.

Michael Galvin's book, *Black blight*, is a compelling account of the Famine in the parishes of Kilmichael, Kilmurry, Newcestown and Enniskeane in west Cork. These parishes were incorporated into three poor law unions – Macroom, Bandon and Dunmanway. Galvin maps the demographic, social, economic and agricultural changes that occured before, during and after the Famine. Both Galvin and Patrick Hickey address religious controversy during the Famine as proselytism, or more commonly souperism (food for conversion), was evident in west Cork. A disagreement between the two authors arises over an incident in the parish of Kilmoe. Galvin claims that the Catholic priest fled the parish while Revd Fisher, a Protestant rector, stayed with and fed the people. Hickey strongly disputes this view and holds that the parish priest, Revd Laurence O'Sullivan, did not abandon his flock but rather went to the diocesan seminary in Cork to highlight the plight of his famine-ravaged parish. Furthermore, Hickey asserts that the longest O'Sullivan could have been away for is nine days and the purpose of his absence was to raise subscriptions for food in order to counter Fisher's souperism. Both Galvin and Hickey agree that the vast majority of clergy of both persuasions gave relief freely without any preconditions as their ultimate aim was to save lives.

Skibbereen: the Famine story is the title of a book and walking trail app by local historians, Terri Kearney and Philip O'Regan. This latest addition to the historiography of the Famine in Skibbereen reaches new levels in terms of technology, which brings the horrific events of this era to life. The book is carefully crafted with informative maps and illustrations. This compliments the walking trail app as the reader can retrace the steps taken by our forebears. The story is about people and places and the authors' aim is to make the history of the famine accessible to a wide audience.

The historiography of the Great Famine in west Cork omits Kinsale. Unlike Skibbereen, Kinsale did not receive notoriety from the press and this among other factors may have led to a belief that Kinsale and district escaped the worst ravages of the Famine. However, research proves otherwise. This book on the Great Famine in Kinsale attempts to contribute to understanding the extent of suffering the people of Kinsale and the surrounding area endured during the mid-1840s and early 1850s.

The research is primarily based on the archives of the Kinsale board of guardians – minute books, indoor relief registers, record of deaths book, fever hospital patients' register – and local sources such as the unpublished annals of the Sisters of Mercy, Kinsale. The British parliamentary papers, newspapers and the relief commission papers are also used.

The starting point for any study on the Great Famine is the pre-Famine era and the first chapter provides an insight into pre-Famine conditions in Kinsale from a social and economic perspective. The state of the fisheries and agriculture in the area is discussed and the living conditions of the poor are assessed. The Poor Law – introduced for the relief of the poor in 1838 – and the role of the workhouse is examined in the pre-Famine era.

The second chapter discusses the calamity that brought devastation to the people of Kinsale and surrounding countryside. The arrival of the potato blight in 1845 marked the beginning of the Great Famine in Kinsale. Although Kinsale was severely hit by the blight in the first year the relief measures introduced by the government and the efforts of the local relief committees, charitable organizations and individuals kept famine at bay. By the autumn of 1846, Kinsale had suffered a second potato crop failure with almost a total wipe out of the crop. The responses from Lord John Russell's government, which made public works the main vehicle for relief, had a devastating effect on a debilitated population. This increased the burden on charitable organizations in the provision of food to the poor. By January 1847, the spiralling cost of food and inadequate wages meant the consequences of famine were evident in Kinsale. Deaths from starvation were beginning to occur and a range of infectious diseases were gripping the population. The incidental appearance of Asiatic cholera in 1849 dramatically increased suffering and mortality in Kinsale union. The medical officers in Kinsale were overwhelmed by the scale and severity of the Great Famine. They were unable and ill-equipped to stem the tide of death and disease. A detailed analysis of the medical response to the Famine in Kinsale is provided.

From August 1847, an extended poor law became responsible for all famine relief in Kinsale union. This brought Kinsale workhouse to the forefront of relief measures for the remainder of the Great Famine. The third chapter examines the living conditions in the workhouse and auxiliary wards and critically analyses the responses from the poor law guardians to the high number of deaths recorded. Finally, this study concludes by giving an overview of the Great Famine in Kinsale and the impact it had on the lives of the people.

1. Pre-Famine Kinsale

It was above all the poverty of such a large segment of the Irish population that made the great famine so destructive of human life.[1]

In the early 19th century Ireland was viewed by the English as a rebellious, under-developed, lawless country.[2] Pre-Famine Ireland became the subject of intense scrutiny by the British parliament. After the Act of Union in 1801, numerous commissions of inquiry were formed to establish the social and economic condition of the country. These reports supported the view that Ireland was backward, poverty-stricken and over populated.[3] This chapter aims to give an insight into the pre-Famine conditions in Kinsale, in order to assess the scale, severity and impact of the Great Famine on the people.

Kinsale is situated on the south coast of county Cork, 12 miles from Bandon and 16 miles south-west of Cork city. In 1843, Kinsale was 'a post, market, and sea-port town, and a parliamentary borough'.[4] A military barracks was located at Charles Fort, east of the town, with 16 officers and 332 non-commissioned officers and privates, who were commanded by a governor and a fort major. Kinsale district was served by eight coast-guard stations, the principal one located at Old Head, comprising a force of eight officers and 63 men under the supervision of an inspecting commander. A constabulary force was stationed in the town to maintain law and order and there was a borough gaol to accommodate prisoners. Kinsale was a corporation town and the business of the corporation as well as the courts of record and session were held in the townhall throughout the year. Kinsale had well established systems of law and order and a long history of local government that ran contrary to the English perception of Ireland as a lawless country.

The main trade in Kinsale town was the fishery, with an approximate value of £30,000 per annum. Agriculture was the staple in the rural areas of the barony and neighbouring baronies of Kinalea, Kerrycurrihy and Courceys. The trade of the port was principally in the export of agricultural produce, with imports of timber, coal, iron and salt. Samuel Lewis, topographer, noted that the trade of the port was 'inconsiderable in proportion to its local advantages' because of its proximity to the port of Cork. Although Kinsale benefited economically during the Napoleonic wars, when the port was a meeting point for large squadrons of the British navy, trade diminished after the wars ended.[5]

Connectivity to the hinterland and markets was by road or sea and the only public transport available was the mail-coach to Cork.[6] A bridge over the river Bandon was proposed to provide direct access to the rich agricultural districts along the south-west coast, which would promote the trade and prosperity of the town. To this end, the people of Kinsale subscribed £4,000, of an estimated £9,000 cost, towards the erection of the bridge. However, the government refused assistance and the project was abandoned.[7] Another setback to trade was the decline in Kinsale's brewing industry during the 1840s. This was mainly due to the temperance movement, founded by Revd Theobald Mathew in the 1830s in a bid to change the social habits of the Irish.[8]

Notwithstanding a decline in certain industries, many were thriving. Milling was an important industry in the Kinsale district. In 1832, a new mill was built in the nearby town of Belgooly at a cost of £7,000. The mill was equipped with the 'most modern machinery' and was capable of producing 15,000 bags of flour annually. A vinegar distillery and a starch-potato mill were also located in Belgooly.[9] Kinsale had a growing tourism industry with facilities such as hot and cold sea-water baths and airy and comfortable lodgings. Moreover, the nearby marine villages of Scilly and Cove (Summercove) attracted large numbers of visitors.[10] A fine hotel, the Royal George, was located on the Long-quay and nearby there was 'a handsome suite' of assembly-rooms for the reception of visitors.[11] On the eve of the Famine, Kinsale had a diverse economy that could hardly be called backward.

Another factor influencing the social and economic conditions of the country was population and its relationship to poverty.[12] Between the mid-18th century and 1845, Ireland's population increased from around 2.6 million to 8.5 million, with widespread poverty 'more acute in the west and parts of the south'.[13] Moreover, the majority of the population were almost completely dependent on a single crop – the potato – for their existence.[14] This upward trend in population was not reflected in Kinsale, as the town's population declined from 7,312 in 1831[15] to 6,182 in 1841.[16] During the 1830s there is evidence from the various royal commission reports that Kinsale was an area of high emigration, and this may have contributed to the population decline.

Pre-Famine poverty exhibited strong regional and even local dimensions in relation to housing and literacy. This was evident in the barony of Kinsale and was highlighted by the 1841 census. The census data showed a wide gap in literacy levels and living conditions between the town and rural areas of the barony. Out of a total population of 12,947 in the barony of Kinsale, 6,996 persons aged five and over could neither read nor write. In Kinsale town 2,717 persons aged five and over were illiterate and this number increased to 4,279 in the rural areas of the barony.[17] This variation may have been due to better educational opportunities in Kinsale town. In 1843, there were two Protestant Sunday schools, a Roman Catholic Sunday school and six daily schools with an attendance of 577 children.[18] In 1844 a convent was established in Kinsale and the Sisters of Mercy opened a school 'to provide religious and literary education' for the poor children of the town, which would further widen the gap between town and rural literacy levels.[19]

Pre-Famine Kinsale

However, the most extensive and striking variation in poverty was in the area of housing. The 1841 census identified four types of houses with the poorest in society living in the lowest or fourth-class houses. These were wretched dwellings: one-roomed cabins, windowless and made of mud. Third-class houses were cottages made of mud but varying from two-to-four rooms with windows. Good farm and town houses were in the second-class category and all dwellings of a better description than the previous three classes were categorized as first-class.[20]

Table 1. Statistics for housing in the barony of Kinsale, 1841: number and proportion of families in each class of house, in Kinsale town and rural areas of barony[21]

Class	Number (town)	Proportion	Number (rural)	Proportion
1st	236	17%	32	3%
2nd	789	56%	188	16%
3rd	375	26%	418	36%
4th	17	1%	521	45%
Total	1417	100%	1159	100%

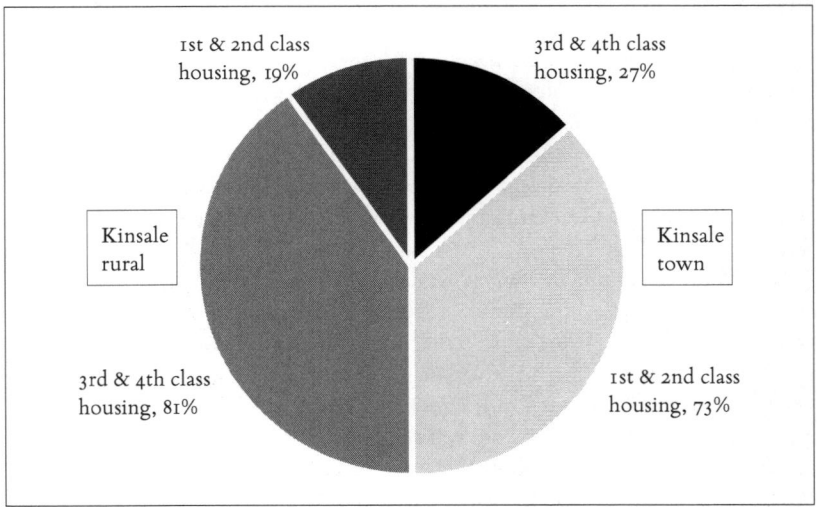

2. Local variations in housing, 1841 (based on table 1)

The rural area of Kinsale barony exhibited a pyramidal social structure with 81 per cent of families living in poor housing as outlined in figure 2. In Ireland, 83.5 per cent of the rural population lived in poor housing and this trend is reflected in the housing statistics for Kinsale. In contrast, Kinsale town did not conform to the pyramidal structure or to housing statistics for the larger towns in Ireland, where 33.9 and 36.7 per cent of families lived in third and fourth-class houses respectively.[22] Only one per cent of families in Kinsale town lived in the lowest category, with 26 per cent living in third-class houses.

Table 1 shows the prosperity of Kinsale town, taking housing as an indicator given the number of families living in first- and second-class houses. However, contemporaneous descriptions of the town's dwellings emphasized the divide between rich and poor. The *Parliamentary Gazetteer of Ireland* compared the picturesqueness of the mansions on Compass Hill to the shabby and miserable houses on the narrow streets below. Moreover, estimating variations in poverty between urban and rural areas is more complex, based on the 1841 census alone, as evidence given to the Poor Inquiry and Devon commission established.

In 1833, the British government set up a commission to investigate the conditions of the poorer classes in Ireland. The function of the commissioners under the chairmanship of Archbishop Whately of Dublin was to establish the type of relief already provided and recommend remedial measures to improve the conditions of the Irish poor. The commissioners were more sympathetic to the plight of the Irish poor and the findings bleaker than the British government had anticipated. The core finding in the report was an acknowledgment that state intervention was essential, but relief based on the English poor law model was unsuitable for Ireland. The recommendations put forward by the commissioners were unpalatable to the British establishment. Assisted emigration and state-sponsored economic development, such as land reclamation and development of the fisheries would require financial support. The orientation of the report was contrary to the political thinking of the time, a *laissez faire* outlook that opposed interference by the government in a market economy and after three years of conscientious enquiries into the condition of the Irish poor the report was shelved.[23]

The Poor Inquiry did, however, highlight the social conditions of the poor, as the commissioners interviewed witnesses throughout the country. In the parish of St Multose, town of Kinsale, 12 people gave evidence to the inquiry, all of high standing in the parish.[24] Hence, the extent and causes of poverty were explored from the viewpoint of the upper classes.

In the pre-Famine era, begging was a survival mechanism that compelled the disadvantaged to rely on random charity in the absence of any legal entitlement to poor relief.[25] In Kinsale there were nearly 100 regular beggars living in the town, which was described by a witness 'as a parish swarming with beggars'. In addition, migrant beggars reduced to vagrancy from unemployment, such as the Bandon weavers and Lord Carbery's evicted tenants from his Castlefreke estate, came to Kinsale to beg. A contributing factor to vagrancy in Kinsale was food shortages, especially in the hungry months when stocks of potatoes were exhausted, forcing many agricultural labourers and vagrants into the towns in search of food. In addition, seasonal unemployment in the fishery increased vagrancy in the town.[26]

Poverty among the 'regular town-beggars' was endemic with most of them suffering from a disability. The majority of Kinsale beggars were old women and widows, with 'some old men'. There were 'very few sturdy beggars'. Despite their destitution and wretched living conditions many beggars were resilient to disease and very few died of cholera 'in proportion with other [poorer] classes'. Deaths from starvation were rare but they suffered and died from 'bad and insufficient food'. In Kinsale the only type of relief available was charity; money was given by the gentry and shopkeepers, and food by the lower classes. Begging generated an income of 6d. or 7d. a week and a diet of broken meat after family dinners supported the beggar and his family. In the countryside farmers were generous towards beggars giving them food and potatoes. Although some cases of deception occurred – as beggars hoarded money and wore rags to obtain alms – most of them led miserable lives.[27]

One of the poorest groups in Irish society was subsistent women.[28] However, there was no relief available to destitute women, orphans or illegitimate children in Kinsale. These women had few employment opportunities, with the widows of fishermen 'more numerous than those of any other class'. Labourers' widows were in a similar situation and were at the mercy of the landlord who usually evicted them. This vulnerable group were mostly supported by their neighbours and friends, but some were reduced to begging. One witness observed that 'it is a mystery to me how they live; most of them must half starve themselves'.[29]

In Kinsale the vast majority of the elderly poor were supported by their relatives and neighbours. American relatives also provided some remittances, but many others who were not so fortunate resorted to seeking alms for subsistence. An institution known as the Gift house that was supported by the Southwell family provided a remittance of 2s. weekly for eight widows of deceased Protestant tradesmen. In addition, there was one almshouse for Protestants, containing 16 rooms for the elderly poor, and these received an allowance from church funds.[30] The Roman Catholic aged and infirm were not 'regularly supported by the gentry or by money collected at the chapel', prompting one witness to state that 'the charity of the poor to each other is wonderfully great'.[31]

Poverty and health were closely linked, with endemic poverty having a detrimental effect on the health and welfare of a population.[32] In pre-Famine Kinsale, medical charities, institutions comprising of a dispensary, fever hospital and an infirmary, were in place to provide medical relief for the sick poor. In addition, there was a network of dispensaries in the locality – Ballinhassig, Ballinspittle, Carrigaline, Dunderrow and Oysterhaven – that offered gratuitous medical advice and medicines.[33] Medical charities were funded by local subscriptions and the grand jury cess. These partially funded public health institutions were the first welfare provisions available in the pre-Famine era.

Besides the medical charities in Kinsale, the only assistance afforded to the sick poor was from the Sick Room-Keepers' Society of Kinsale. This philanthropic organization was motivated by strong religious sentiment. Sectarian tensions surfaced at the Poor Inquiry when the parish priest, Revd Justin McNamara, made an allegation that the Society's chief objective was proselytism. He claimed that the Society's members withdrew assistance when a sick person refused religious instruction. However, the accusation of proselytism was vigorously refuted by another witness, Mr King Nason, who stated that the objective of the Society was to 'relieve distress'. He added:

> Of course the visitors conceive it their first duty to read the word of God for every poor suffering creature, but if it is objected to, they do not persist; and they do not refuse or withdraw relief on account of refusal to hear them.[34]

The Society provided 50 to 60 people with a weekly supply of coals, bread, meal or groceries. The sick poor were afforded relief from the Society, but only to those they deemed worthy of receiving it.

Despite the relief accessible to the sick poor the best support available was from the poor themselves. One witness asserted that 'the poor willingly assist each other when afflicted with any contagious disease' even the dreaded cholera. Moreover, unemployment was also a consequence of sickness. There were no friendly or benefit clubs where the sick poor could obtain relief when unemployed and they often had to send what they possessed to the pawn-shop or ask for alms, which led them into a life of mendicancy. The Catholic curate, Revd Walsh, described the wretchedness of the poor:

> The misery to which the poor are sometimes reduced is frightful; last Christmas I was called out to visit a poor man; I found him lying with no covering but a piece of old torn carpet; the straw under him was almost turned to dirt; there were five or six children about him; they did not beg, but were actually starving, this poor man was thrown out of work through sickness; some persons who heard of this case, relieved him.[35]

One of the causal factors of poverty among the lower classes was unemployment. However, relief for the able-bodied unemployed was viewed with a degree of scepticism by those in authority. In Kinsale the labouring poor and fishermen constituted this category. The inquiry heard evidence on the very improvident and intemperate habits of the fishermen in Kinsale. These were deemed the undeserving poor, as a perception existed that poverty in this group was a result of idleness, vice or recklessness. Around 300 fishermen were employed throughout the year on first-class, hooker-sailing boats and earned on average between 8*s*. and 9*s*. a week. A few of these fishermen were comfortable but the majority of them led wretched lives. According to one witness:

> When they get a large payment, they go at once to the whiskey shop; and when fish is scarce, and their weekly income little, they are sometimes

almost starving, pawning their very jackets to get food ... they could easily provide ... for their widows and orphans; but they make no provision for anything.[36]

This recklessness led them into a life of misery and destitution as the witness blamed the living and social conditions of these fishermen on 'their infatuation in getting drunk'. Poverty was high among 'the remainder' of the fishermen in Kinsale as they only had seasonal employment in the fishery. This group consisted of around 120 'Seiners' and about an equal number of drift-net fishermen who went out in inferior boats. They earned on average 4s. to 5s. a week from fishing and many of them worked part-time as labourers. Almost all of them had a potato garden, but they suffered great distress due to the shortage of food when their potatoes were exhausted. This forced their wives and children into the countryside to beg. Although 'the potatoes are often given from charity', they were not classified as regular beggars as they always tried to give tobacco, pins and needles or something small in return.[37]

The unemployed labouring classes also suffered food shortages and were 'reduced to few and very scanty meals for their subsistence'. Revd McNamara outlined the consequences of unemployment on the labouring classes:

> Though there are not many destitute in the strict sense of the word, there is an immense number in a most wretched condition, they have food, but of a bad kind and quite insufficient in quantity ... The labouring classes (particularly in the country) are often obliged to eat a sort of potatoes which I verily believe would be rank poison if their constitutions were not accustomed to it.[38]

According to both Roman Catholic clergymen at the inquiry, early marriages were the norm in Kinsale. This added more pressure on the social conditions of the poor. The clergy tried to avert early marriages by explaining to the couples the added burden of a family on their resources. However, the priests asserted that they could 'not refuse to perform the ceremony' as the poor must be preserved 'from as much vice as possible'. The clergy's moral obligations took precedence over the material well-being of the poor and the consequences were overcrowding and poor living conditions, as Revd McNamara stated:

> Commonly a whole family, sometimes two or three families live in one room ... I have frequently found a room inhabited where the rain came in through the walls and broken roof. There are many without bed-clothes; they are obliged to lie down in the clothes they have worn all day, and these are often wet. There is seldom any regular bedding, they [poor] do not think of providing such a thing; they lie on a little straw, which is rarely changed; I have sometimes seen it so broken into pieces by repeated shiftings as to be almost powder.[39]

The constant struggle for subsistence among the poor meant that they never provided for the future as it was a struggle for them to accomplish mere survival.

While the Poor Inquiry primarily focused on the town of Kinsale, a royal commission, known as the Devon commission, set up to inquire into the occupation of land in Ireland, concentrated on the rural community. The Devon commission met in Kinsale on 12 September 1844 and heard evidence from five local people, representing the baronies of Kinsale, Kerrycurrihy and Kinalea. Three of the respondents were resident landlords and two were large tenant farmers who gave an insight into the social and economic conditions of the rural population in the Kinsale area, albeit from an upper-class viewpoint. Details were given on the general state of agriculture, crops, farm size, emigration, wages and the land tenure system.

According to Thomas Herrick, Kinalea landlord, agriculture in the area was a mixture of tillage and dairy. He thought that farming practices had improved with the introduction of the Scottish swing plough and attributed this to the farming society in the Kinsale union. However, he noted that the society was 'confined to the gentry'.[40] The main crops grown in Kinsale union were potatoes and wheat. Michael Forrest, tenant farmer from Lisclery parish, estimated that on good soil, an acre of ground produced 768 weights of potatoes and 120 stone of wheat.[41] The prominence of Kinsale as a major potato growing area was achieved by the availability and use of sea manure, land reclamation and access to markets.[42] Furthermore, the large number of mills in the district denoted the importance of the wheat crop to the local economy.

However, as agriculture was improving slowly for the big farmers, it was deteriorating for the small farmers, cottiers and labourers. William Herrick, Innishannon landlord, explained that two townlands on his estate were 'held by long leases under middlemen, and they are the worst part – the most pauperized and the worse tilled'. Furthermore, he stated that once the middlemen's leases expired farms were consolidated. Thus, the fate of the numerous occupying tenants was eviction and only the 'best tenantry' were kept. Emigration was an option but only for a class able to pay for themselves. Herrick asserted that emigration from the area was not encouraged, as it 'was so great that, at one time, this district was very much in want of labourers'. Thomas Herrick claimed that labourers' conditions had improved. He believed that evictions after consolidation of farms did not cause any hardship as the evicted tenants either went to America or became labourers and were 'more comfortable than before'.[43]

Contradictory evidence was given by William Meade, Ballymartle landlord, on the social conditions of labourers. He thought that 'labourers under the ordinary class of farmer' were not improving; 'their houses are very wretched indeed' and the agreement between the farmer and labourer was 'not a money matter'. The lack of wage labour and steady work left the labourer in a precarious position. Michael Forrest confirmed Meade's view of the small farmers' and labourers' living standards, stating that 'they live very poorly ... on the dry horse potato'. However, if they had a cow for milk and fish in season as well as potatoes then their diet improved, but in some seasons 'they must and do live on dry potatoes'. A labourer's wages ranged from 6*d*. a day with diet to 8*d*. a day, and the rent for an acre of land for one growing season ranged from £4 to £8 depending on the type of manure used. Furthermore, he paid an additional £1 to 30*s*. for his cabin. This was a handsome profit for the farmer as the average rent in the Kinsale district was 15*s*. to £1 per acre. The lack of leases and rents fixed on a yearly basis, by proposal rather than by land valuation, led to insecurity of tenure. Furthermore, subdivision still occurred in the area with 'a very general anxiety among persons to divide the land among their sons'. Michael Forrest claimed that some small farmers 'labour incessantly and live as poorly' as labourers. While the lower classes were getting poorer, all five respondents were of the view that the larger farmers were getting richer.[44] In the rural communities, as in the town of Kinsale, poverty was a matter of class.[45]

Poverty in Ireland presented the government with a dilemma once they decided not to adopt the recommendations of the poor inquiry. They still required some poor relief measures that 'could be implemented quickly and cheaply' and help Ireland become a more stable and productive society. George Nicholls, English poor law commissioner, was despatched with a view to extending the 1834 English poor law to Ireland. Nicholls concluded that the workhouse model, with a test of destitution to avoid abuse, could be administered in Ireland. These findings were incorporated into the 1838 Poor Law act that divided Ireland into 130 unions. Each union had a workhouse at its centre, supported by a local poor rate and administered by a board of poor law guardians. These were supervised and controlled by assistant commissioners based in Ireland, with overall responsibility for the poor law assigned to the English poor law commissioners.[46]

Kinsale poor law union was formally declared on 30 January 1839, covering an area of 121 square miles, with a population of 41,929 in 1831.[47] There were seven ex-officio and 21 elected guardians, the latter mainly local landlords representing their electoral divisions. Kinsale union broadly encompassed the baronies of Kinalea, Kinsale, Kerrycurrihy and Courceys, which consisted of sixteen electoral divisions – Ballyfeard, Ballyfoyle, Ballymartle, Carrigaline, Cullen, East Courceys, West Courceys, Kilmanogue, Kilpatrick, Kinnure, Kinsale, Leofany, Liscleary, Nohoval, Templebredy and Tracton – with each electoral division responsible for the cost of its paupers. Kinsale workhouse opened on 4 December 1841 and admitted five beggars and one destitute person on that day.[48]

From the outset, the Kinsale board of guardians complained to the poor law commissioners about the cost and size of the workhouse, with a proposed capacity for 500 paupers, they deemed it 'more than double the number ever likely to occupy it'. Furthermore, they cited emigration from the area as a mitigating factor on the numbers likely to apply for relief. The guardians argued that the cost of erecting the workhouse – £5,900 with a further £1,000 for fittings and furnishings – was too expensive and not in proportion to the rateable properties due to the smallness of the union.[49] In the pre-Famine era, the low number of admissions, shown in figure 3, reflects the reluctance of the poor to resort to the workhouse for relief.

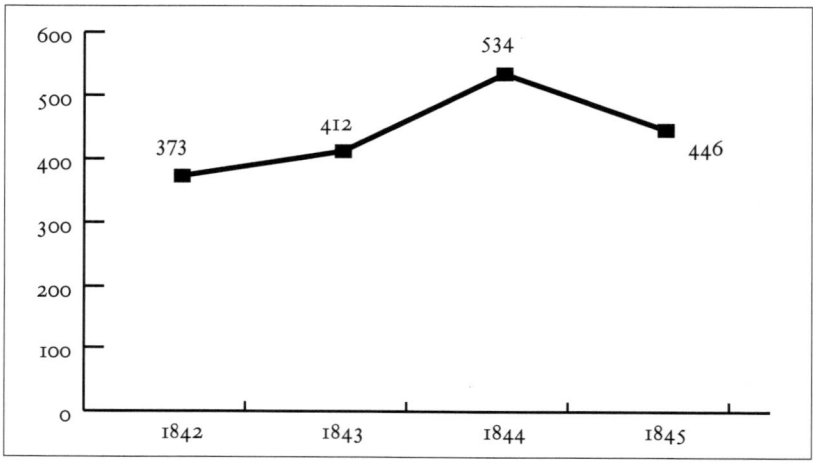

3. Yearly admissions to Kinsale workhouse, 1842–5[50]

However, some of the more vulnerable groups did seek relief in Kinsale workhouse. Between 17 December 1841 and 30 September 1845, the majority of those admitted were women and children under twelve years. Beggars and migrant paupers, who were not resident in any particular electoral division and were charged to the general union, also entered the workhouse (fig. 4).

A conclusion may be drawn that the workhouse system provided relief for those it was designed for; a place of last resort for the destitute with punitive deterrents in place to prevent entry. Paupers had to undergo a test of destitution and relief was only available inside the workhouse. The severity of the workhouse test was evident by the low number of fishermen who entered the workhouse, a group identified by the poor inquiry as bordering on destitution. From 1842 to 1845, around 38 fishermen were admitted to the workhouse and at least 10 of them were repeat entrants. Around 24 fishermen were aged 60 and over and the majority of them were classified as aged and infirm, or with some form of disability or ailment. Only two fishermen in the group were categorized as able-bodied.[51]

The administration of the workhouse was based on strict adherence to discipline and order; individuals could not enter unless their entire families entered with them. Segregation of men, women and children took place

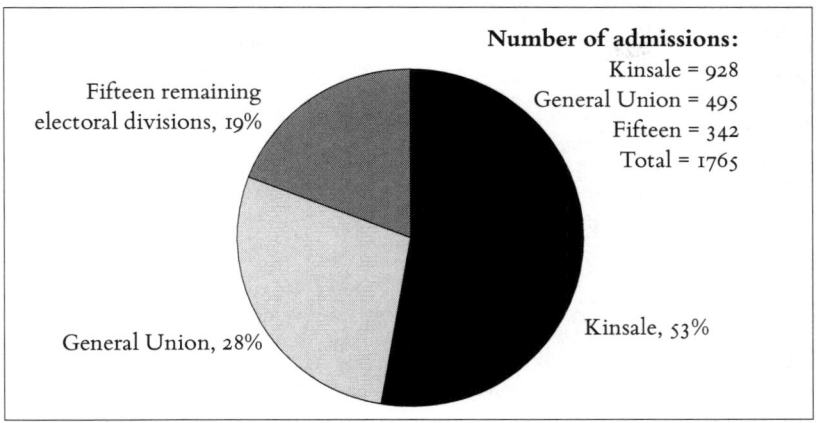

4. Proportion of inmates across electoral divisions, 1842–5

upon entry and a diet that was inferior to that of the lowest labourer outside the workhouse was part of the disincentives enforced to keep applicants to a minimum.[52] Kinsale board of guardians complied with the intentions of the poor law and the stringency of the workhouse test deterred entry.

On the eve of the Great Famine, Kinsale was beginning to prosper as social and economic conditions improved. The town enjoyed unparalleled living standards compared to towns of a similar size in Ireland. Kinsale was a 'lively' fishing town and a new industry – tourism – was emerging.[53] In the rural areas of Kinsale union agriculture was slowly improving and a wide range of agricultural products were exported. A limited form of social welfare was introduced by the poor law and medical charities provided relief to the sick poor. However, improvements were mainly confined to the upper classes and in Kinsale prosperity and poverty existed side by side. Poverty was endemic among the lower classes and their reliance on the potato crop for subsistence made them dangerously dependent on one food source.

2. Famine, death and disease in Kinsale Union

The proximate cause of the Great Irish Famine (1846–52) was the fungus Phytophthora infestans *(or potato blight), which reached Ireland in the autumn of 1845.*[1]

THE ARRIVAL OF THE POTATO BLIGHT

The role of the potato in the pre-Famine Irish diet was undisputed, providing the staple food for more than half the population.[2] By 1845 the danger of overdependence on potatoes, as a single food source, was evident as previous food shortages in 1817, 1822, 1831, 1839 and 1842 highlighted the need for relief measures to prevent starvation.[3] Moreover, the Irish peasant was accustomed to scarcity during the hungry months of June, July and August, when the old potatoes were exhausted and the new crop was not ready to harvest.

Over the first half of the 19th century the variety of potato grown had changed from traditional varieties, such as the apple, to the lumper potato. The apple was of a very high quality compared to the lumper, with the latter grown for its productivity on poor soil and its resistance to diseases, such as wart disease and leaf roll. The high-yielding crop and relative ease with which it grew made the lumper the poor man's diet.[4] However, its lack of quality was outweighed by the quantity of potatoes consumed, typically up to 14 lbs. per day for an adult male labourer and proportionally less for women and children.[5] Potatoes eaten with skimmed milk or buttermilk provided all of the nutrients for an almost perfect diet. Thus, this food source provided sustenance to the majority of the population. The importance of the potato extended even further than human consumption, as it was used for animal feed, especially for pigs, thereby contributing to agricultural output.[6]

By the late summer and early autumn of 1845 a new potato disease had spread throughout Europe. The fungal disease *Phytophthora infestans*, commonly known as potato blight, was first noticed in Cork around the second week of September. The mould fungus grew on the underside of potato plant leaves and produced fungal spores, which were then transmitted by air and water. Once the spores settled on new plants the process of destruction resumed. The disease was extremely virulent, as the spores infected the tubers below ground.[7] From mid-September, many newspapers carried differing reports on the potato disease. According to the *Leinster Express*, 'there was never a finer poor man's harvest. The oats and potatoes are most luxuriant'. The *Sligo Journal* reported that in some districts the potato crop 'promises well', whereas in other areas there were many complaints of 'a rot in the ground'.[8] As the appearance of blight was sporadic rather than universal and for various other reasons, such as the large acreage sown in 1845, early public opinion on the state of the potato crop was restrained.[9] Nonetheless, much uneasiness existed among farmers in the districts where the potato disease manifested itself.[10]

Reports of the blight prompted the Prime Minister, Sir Robert Peel, to gather data on the state of the potato crop as he feared a disaster if the crop was totally destroyed.[11] Detailed reports were requested from the constabulary, members of the coastguard and boards of poor law guardians to assess the scale of the crop failure. It was only when harvesting began, in October, that the extent of the loss was fully realized. These reports confirmed the sporadic nature of the disease and that some areas were affected far more than others. In 1845, Co. Cork had 250,000 acres under potatoes, with Kinsale district a major producer.[12] It was clear from the reports that the Kinsale area had suffered a heavy loss. On 29 October 1845 a constabulary report gave a pessimistic view on the state of the crop:

> Potatoes that were apparently sound have become diseased. More than one-quarter of the crop in this district may be considered lost at present. Out of 12 acres of apple potatoes at Carrigaline (average value 72 guineas per acre), the proprietor does not expect to get £1 for the portion remaining sound. The people are following advice and making every effort to preserve the sound and recover the tainted.[13]

In late November, Kinsale board of guardians reported on the extent of the potato disease in their respective districts. They came to the conclusion that the potato crop affected by the disease varied between one-half to one-third, except in one district where it amounted to one-quarter. Furthermore, the guardians reported that alarm was spreading among the labouring classes who relied 'wholly' on the potato for food and support. This report highlighted that Kinsale union was after suffering a heavy crop loss from the blight. Under these circumstances the Board urged the government to adopt measures by procuring a supply of food for the poor, in order to relieve the inevitable distress that would occur in the following spring.[14]

As reports of the blight were unfolding, Peel's Conservative government responded by establishing a scientific commission to investigate the cause and suggest remedies to halt the progress of the disease. The three member commission consisted of a Scottish chemist, Dr Lyon Playfair, an Irish scientist, Sir Robert Kane, and the renowned botanist Dr John Lindley who was editor of the *Gardeners' Chronicle* and *Agricultural Gazette*. The commissioners failed to identify the cause of the disease. They did, however, put forward proposals for the use of diseased potatoes, as well as various recommendations for the storage of sound potatoes to try and salvage the crop. However, the remedies were unsuccessful.[15]

The government's next initiative was to establish a temporary Relief Commission, which was to advise on the levels of distress, organize food depots and oversee the formation and co-ordinate the activities of local relief committees. At the same time, Peel had arranged for the secret importation of £100,000 worth of Indian corn from America, to be stored in depots around the country. In December 1845, Peel's final measure was an additional grant of money to the Board of Public Works, which was intended for employment on small works of utility. However, a clear distinction was made by the government between the extraordinary or temporary measures that Peel introduced to meet the crisis and the permanent relief measures in place to provide for ordinary destitution under the 1838 Poor Law act.[16]

Kinsale board of guardians were responsible for the relief of ordinary destitution in Kinsale union. However, they were concerned that the destitution resulting from the crop failure in the district would put a strain on their resources. At the weekly board meeting on 30 October 1845, preparations were made to secure a supply of food in anticipation of the scarcity and the visiting committee was requested to buy a few tons of meal and storage bins from Cork. In order to maximize the amount of food available, one of the recommendations from the scientific commission was the manufacture of starch from diseased potatoes. This would make use of the potatoes while starch mixed with meal or flour could be used to make bread. The Kinsale board of guardians adopted this recommendation and proposed to construct 'a mill according to the plan contained in the *Gardeners' Chronicle*'. The master of the workhouse was directed to buy '200 weights of diseased potatoes' and a starch-making machine. Any sound portion of the diseased potatoes was to be boiled and used as part of the workhouse diet. The starch machine cost 15s. 8d. However, there is no evidence that starch was made from diseased potatoes in the workhouse and this project is likely to have been abandoned.[17]

In November 1845 the poor law commissioners permitted a departure from a potato-based workhouse diet.[18] Thus, the first effect of the potato blight in Kinsale workhouse was on the pauper's diet. On 11 December 1845 the guardians directed the master to 'give stirabout for breakfast instead of potatoes and to change from milk to porridge for dinner in future'.[19]

By mid-December 1845 a constabulary report stated that up to three-quarters of the potato crop was lost in some districts of Kinsale union and around one-third of the labourers were unemployed.[20] However, Lieutenant Joseph Irwin, Kinsale coastguard, reported that it was difficult to obtain correct information with regard to the scarcity. He could only hope that the diseased potatoes were not getting worse and recommended feeding them to cattle and pigs rather than throwing them out.[21] Reports with conflicting views and confusion around the cause of the potato disease marked the first six months of the Great Famine, which caused tardiness in government responses.

One of the first responses to scarcity in a community is the movement of people in search of food and work.[22] This was a major concern for the Kinsale guardians as persons on the verge of pauperism came into the town in search of employment. They feared that many paupers would then be compelled to seek relief in the workhouse, thereby 'throwing an unjust portion of expense on this house' and in particular the ratepayers of Kinsale electoral division. A motion of uniformity for the maintenance of paupers within the union, in order to equalize the cost of paupers among all electoral divisions, was proposed by Dr Daunt, one of the Kinsale guardians. However, the motion would have added an extra cost to the ratepayers in the rural electoral divisions and only benefited the ratepayers of Kinsale. In the interest of fairness to the rural guardians, Mr Knolles put forward a motion to rescind the resolution as many electoral divisions were unrepresented at the meeting.[23]

By the spring of 1846, potatoes had become scarce and expensive. In Kinsale, the price of potatoes had almost doubled from 3½d. in September 1845 to 6¼d. by the following March.[24] This resulted in the guardians issuing an order not to purchase any potatoes after an estimated five-week stock ran out and to save the existing stock by serving potatoes at one meal only per day. The guardians requested the commissioners to furnish them with a recommendation for an alternative cheap food source due to the high cost of potatoes.[25] On 10 April 1846, J. Hosford, clerk of Kinsale union, ordered one ton of Indian meal for the workhouse from the government depot in Cork.[26] The poor law commissioners were concerned that the guardians were opting for Indian meal, provided at a fixed price by the government, rather than relying on private traders to supply their demand. They urged the guardians to induce the farmers to bring their potatoes to the market at a reasonable rate.[27] This would conserve the government's food supplies and reduce the hoarding of potatoes.

Although outdoor relief was forbidden under the poor law, by March 1846, Mr Daunt recognized the distress caused by the shortage and cost of potatoes in the union. He called the Board's attention to the issue and recommended 'taking steps to provide food for cases of distress within this union, independent of inmate relief'.[28] Moreover, the scarcity impacted some parishes within Kinsale union more than others. In the parish of Dunderrow, a local Protestant clergyman, Revd J.B. Webb, called for the immediate distribution of Indian meal to the poor.[29] He blamed absentee landlords for the destitution in the area, as by early April the potatoes in the parish were almost 'entirely exhausted' leaving the poor with no other food source.[30] Consequently, the first victims of dearth in Kinsale union came from the badly managed estates of absentee landlords. Other areas within Kinsale union fared better than Dunderrow, as distress was mitigated by some local landlords who provided for their tenants. In the parish of Ballymartle, William Meade undertook 'to keep all the potatoes grown on his estate for his tenants', thereby reducing the numbers that were likely to seek relief in the workhouse.[31]

By the spring of 1846, measures that the government had initiated in 1845 to meet the crisis were slowly being implemented. The relief commission established in November 1845 was re-organized in January 1846 under the chairmanship of Sir Randolph Routh. Coordination of expenditure on relief was channelled through Charles Trevelyan, assistant-secretary to the treasury, with Routh supervising the distribution of relief in Ireland.[32] The policy of the government was to ensure 'the resources within the reach of the community' were first applied to relieve distress locally and that government aid 'should be only auxiliary to the efforts of the people'.[33]

One of the first tasks the commission undertook was to make arrangements to receive and store the Indian corn that arrived in Ireland from America.[34] In early February, 13 main food depots were established across the country with Cork the main distribution centre. A number of smaller sub-depots were subsequently set up at coastguard stations and at constabulary headquarters.[35] However, the depots were ordered not to open before 15 May 1846, as the treasury's view was that once food aid was given it would be impossible to suspend 'without danger to the public peace'. In addition, the postponement until the latest possible period would ensure self-exertion on the part of the person in want of food.[36] Due to local pressure, sales began at the Cork depot on 28 March 1846, but most did not open until May.

By the beginning of April, distress in the rural areas of Kinsale union was increasing and the local relief committees were still not formed. The *Southern Reporter* made a scathing attack on the government with accusations that the plentiful supplies of food in their depots were 'denied to famishing thousands, who are willing to pay the highest price that government may demand'. The destitute were becoming clamorous and many applicants for food walked from Kinsale to Cork to demand relief.[37]

Local relief committees were slow in forming, as instructions on their formation and duties were not issued by the relief commission until 28 February 1846.[38] Throughout April meetings were held to establish relief committees for the districts of Kinsale, Kerrycurrihy and Kinalea.[39] The committees were made up of local officials, clergy of all persuasions, poor law guardians and other notables in the community, as their local influence and knowledge of the situation made them best-placed to determine the needs of the people and furnish relief without incurring waste. Moreover, it was the government's view that the owners of property and other ratepayers were both legally and morally responsible to provide relief to the destitute poor.[40] On 10 April 1846, Kinsale's relief committee was established under the chairmanship of John Heard and he immediately requested the relief commission to establish a corn depot in the town.[41]

One of the main functions of the relief committees was to raise subscriptions in order to purchase and distribute food in distressed areas. Relief committees could procure food at cost price from government depots but only in cases where there was a scarcity of food within a district or where the price of food was artificially raised. It was never the government's intention to provide food for the poor, rather it was a measure introduced to ease market inflation in times of scarcity. The food was then sold to the poor, and in cases where people were unable to pay for food a task of work was required in return.[42] Gratuitous relief could only be afforded to people incapable of work who had no able-bodied relatives to support them, or when the workhouse was full. However, the government did realize that some assistance was likely to be required in aid of subscriptions. To this end, the treasury provided a grant in proportion to the amount of subscriptions raised, usually two-thirds, though in some distressed areas a grant equal to the amount contributed locally was allocated.[43] In Kinsale union the relief committees received the two-thirds grant as outlined in table 2.

Table 2. Kinsale union relief committees: subscriptions collected locally and government donations received, 1846[44]

Date	Division	Subscription	Donation
25 May 1846	Kinsale	£322 4s. 0d.	£220
3 June 1846	Ballinspittle	£117	£80
8 June 1846	Ballymartle	£86	£60
18 June 1846	Ballyfeard	£118 8s. 6d.	£80
19 June 1846	Carrigaline	£220 17s. 6d.	£140
19 June 1846	Innishannon	£86 1s. 0d.	£60

Government donations made to local committees in aid of subscriptions amounted to around £68,000 by the beginning of August 1846.[45] The grant scheme gave many relief committees the initiative to redouble their efforts in raising subscriptions. In Kinsale union, the Ballinspittle relief committee had received subscriptions totalling £91 0s. 1d., with Captain Alcock Stawell, Kilbrittain Castle, and Lord Kingsale contributing £20 each.[46] However, the chairman, Thomas Cuthbert, was anxious to increase subscriptions in order to maximize the government grant and he directed the secretary to make renewed applications for subscriptions towards the poor relief fund. This appeal was successful with a total amount of £117 subscribed, which demonstrated the good will of the gentry and others to the initial responses of Peel's government to meet the crisis. In addition, many subscribers contributed to more than one relief fund. Captain Stawell subscribed £5 to the Kinsale relief fund and also contributed to the Timoleague fund. Another inducement to subscribers was the acknowledgment in the press of those 'who so generously responded to the call made upon them'.[47]

Opening sub-depots was one of the most successful measures introduced by Peel's government in preventing deaths by starvation along the densely populated south coast. By early June, five sub-depots were open in the Kinsale district. These were located at coastguard stations – Courtmacsherry, Upper

Cove, Old Head, Oyster Haven and Dunny Cove – and were supplied with Indian meal for sale to the distressed population. On 13 June 1846, Routh informed Trevelyan that these small depots on the coast were cost efficient and very effective in the sale and distribution of food. Furthermore, he stated that the benefits of the food depots on the coast extended 'much beyond their own immediate precincts'.[48] In Kinsale union, the food depots at Old Head and Upper Cove enabled the poor to purchase food directly from the coastguards, which alleviated the movement of people into Kinsale town in search of food. However, people needed employment in order to procure food and at a special meeting of the Ballinspittle relief committee, memorials in favour of 'several useful works, which will give extensive employment in the coming summer months' were adopted and forwarded to the lord lieutenant.[49]

Public works, similar to relief committees, were a traditional way to help relieve distress. To this end, Peel's objectives were to relieve immediate distress and also to effect long-term improvements. In March 1846, four pieces of legislation were introduced, to promote the development of piers and harbours, encourage drainage, to make general improvements to estates and for the construction and repair of roads.[50] The method of financing public works was the ultimate decider on works applied for under the legislation. A half-grant scheme was available for road works carried out by the Board of Works, with the other half to be repaid by the local cess over a period of years. Roads sanctioned under the grand jury system were administered locally and loans advanced by the treasury were to be repaid in full. Similarly, works for improvements did not offer any financial incentives as all monies had to be repaid to the government. It was hardly surprising that the attraction of the half-grant scheme made it inevitable that road construction and repair was the preferred option for providing employment. Thus, applications were made to the Board of Works for road works from the baronies of Kinsale, Kinalea and Courceys. The sums of money applied for by each barony were £925, £1,507 6s. 6d. and £180 respectively. Although some road improvements and construction works were sanctioned by the Board of Works for the baronies of Kinalea and Courcies, none were sanctioned for Kinsale during the summer of 1846.[51]

The local relief committees were to play a central role in the administration of employment. Once public works were approved by the Board of Works, it was the responsibility of relief committees to issue tickets for employment to the poor. A particular concern for the commissioners was that tickets were being issued in cases of general distress and not 'urgent and unusual distress arising from the late failure of the potato crop'. On 21 May 1846, Lieutenant-Colonel Jones, chairman of the Board of Public Works, informed Trevelyan that 'farmer, priest, landlord and tenant all make strong attempts to squeeze something out of the government purse'.[52] As a result of the rigorous approval system employed by the Board of Works to weed out exploitation of public works, many schemes were delayed and some were rejected outright.

In early May the Innishannon relief committee forwarded a memorial to the Board of Works from the boatmen of Kinsale and Innishannon, to carry out navigation works on the river Bandon.[53] However, the Board denied funding as these works were outside the auspices of the 'Act' and stated that 'public money could not be spent on a project of such little utility'. The Board, in rejecting the proposal, made a clear distinction between ordinary destitution and the provision of public works to meet the prevailing distress. They stated:

> The committee are employing the most destitute, but there are many fishermen and others in want of employment, which the Board believe is frequently the case in Kinsale, independent of any failure of the food of the people.[54]

Some reproductive works were approved in the rural baronies of Kinalea and Kerrycurrihy where distress was most acute. A report on the drainage of lands, with a list of townlands to be improved and the names of the 'reputed' proprietors was published in the *Cork Examiner*. The Officer of Public Works recommended approval and stated that as well as improving the land for cultivation, the works would provide much wanted employment for the labouring population.[55]

Despite the best efforts of the Board of Works to control the numbers employed there was a dramatic increase over the summer months, reaching a peak of around 98,000 in early August.[56] The reason for this was twofold. First, there was reluctance on the farmers' part to rent conacre due to the difficulty with rent arrears for the previous year. Second, wage labour of around 10d. a day was available on public works.[57] Most farmers operated a wage-labour system leaving the poor with no alternative other than public works to obtain money for food.

The relief measures deployed by Peel's government in the first year of distress were slow to commence and overly bureaucratic. This caused undue distress among the labouring classes. However, once the food depots were opened and public works initiated the relief measures proved effective. The efforts of local relief committees in raising subscriptions and securing employment for the poor, as well as the benevolence of some landlords towards their tenants proved effective in meeting the crisis. Once nothing untoward happened in Kinsale union, then the relief measures would stem the tide of destitution resulting from the first potato crop failure. Unfortunately, this was not the case. The *Gardeners' Chronicle* reported on the reappearance of blight in the new potato crop, with farmers fearing a 'total extinction of the crop' in Kinsale and several other districts.[58] Captain Stawell suggested at the Ballinspittle poor relief committee in May that supplies of seed potatoes be distributed to the poor farmers and cottiers who were unable to procure them. He feared that unless there was a sufficient quantity of potatoes planted the 'privations of the present year ... may be transmitted to the next'.[59]

THE SECOND CROP FAILURE

The total failure of the potato crop in 1846 transformed a temporary crisis into a national calamity. During the summer of 1846, alarm was spreading among the population as accounts of potato blight in the early crop began to appear in the press. In June the Whig government under the leadership of Lord John Russell had replaced Peel's Conservative government. The relief measures introduced by Peel were due to end in mid-August when the new crop of potatoes would become available. The Whig government allowed the temporary relief policies to continue in expectation that all works would close by the end of August.[60]

By August, concerns were growing over the state of the potato crop in Kinsale. A memorial was sent to the lord lieutenant, Lord Bessborough, from members of the Kinsale relief committee outlining that after extensive investigations they had reached a conclusion that the potato crop in the barony of Kinsale was 'altogether lost'. A private letter accompanying the memorial stated: 'There will not be a single potato fit for use ... along the coast from Cork to Clonakilty'.[61]

A complete failure of the potato crop in 1846 was to exacerbate the distress of the poor caused by the partial and localized failure of the 1845 crop. By mid-August the temporary relief measures were winding down and the poor faced another year of distress. This led to social unrest in Kinsale and surrounding areas. A printed notice was posted around the districts of Cork, Kinsale, Bandon and Macroom calling on all labourers and countrymen to a general meeting at Cork Hill, near Ballinhassig, on 15 August 1846. The agenda for the meeting was as follows:

> To take into consideration the present general distress and impending famine occasioned by the total failure of the potato crop and the want of extensive employment, by which our famishing poor could procure food of a different description.

An appeal was made to the landlords and their agents to attend the meeting so that they could witness the distress of the people. Co-operation between the government and landlords was demanded to alleviate the sufferings of the people and check the spread of famine. The notice stated that people attending the meeting should come unarmed and in a peaceful and orderly manner.[62] Nevertheless, the magistrates of Kinsale and surrounding districts became alarmed at the potential for unrest and decided to send troops to marshal the meeting.[63]

Once the second crop failure occurred the traditional relationship between farmers and their bound labourers was disrupted. Farmers were unable to provide food or pay wages to their agricultural labourers, which resulted in the labourers repudiating the agreements that they entered into at the beginning of the season.⁶⁴ According to members of the Kinsale relief committee the breakdown of such relationships endangered the peace of the country. They became alarmed that large assemblies of people had gathered in the town and had threatened proprietors and mill-owners that unless they received immediate relief they would help themselves. The loss of the potato crop meant that wage labour could no longer provide subsistence for the labouring poor and only money wages could offer them some hope of procuring food to prevent starvation. To this end, the Kinsale relief committee urged the government to organize public works on a grand scale to provide employment for the poor and prevent social disorder.⁶⁵

John Heard, chairman of Kinsale relief committee, was angry that the labouring population in the Kinsale district had been unfairly treated. In August, as the temporary relief measures were closing, he complained to the relief commission that public works were not granted – even though presentments of £1,500 were passed – while works were freely sanctioned in neighbouring baronies. Heard warned the commissioners that as the potato crop was totally lost in the barony, 'the time has come when the people must starve or plunder'. After a meeting in Kinsale with angry labourers, he stated: 'They made no secret of their determination to help themselves if they were not able to procure goods by their labour'. According to Heard, social upheaval in Kinsale was the result of the commission's failure to provide employment in the area.⁶⁶

After the complete destruction of the potato crop, it was evident to the Whig government that more relief measures were needed to avert a calamity. The temporary relief measures introduced by Peel were generally deemed to have been successful, in particular the importation of food, which prevented market inflation and provided the poor with cost-price food. However, the Whig government announced a policy of non-interference with the grain trade in the eastern and southern parts of the country, including Kinsale. In the Kinsale district the food depots that played an important role in the previous year's relief measures were not to reopen. An increase in food prices was inevitable and the government, by bowing to the pressure of traders and merchants and sticking to their laissez faire principles, further increased the misery and distress of the people.⁶⁷ Thus the relief committees in Kinsale union were left at the mercy of private merchants to procure food for the poor at spiralling market prices.

According to Lord John Russell the main duty of the government was to provide employment in times of scarcity.⁶⁸ In August 1846 the Whig government introduced a piece of legislation, known as the Labour Rate, that encompassed proposals put forward by Trevelyan.⁶⁹ Public works became the main vehicle for providing relief. Under the act all public works for the employment of the poor were controlled by the Board of Works with the total cost borne by the ratepayers, which centralized control of relief and decentralized funding. Moreover, the type of public works carried out was to be principally unproductive to limit applications on work schemes.⁷⁰

The Labour Rate act did not deter the ratepayers of Kinsale seeking reproductive works that would be advantageous to the area as well as relieving distress. On 2 September 1846, a meeting of highly influential people, consisting of the gentry, clergy and residents of the baronies of Courcies and Kinsale, took place in Kinsale courthouse to memorialize the government for a grant to build a bridge across the river Bandon. The chairman of the meeting, John Heard, outlined the distress that existed in the locality and the need for uniting the two baronies by building a bridge. He predicted:

> There would be upwards of 1,000 persons out of employment – if they were not so already – when the glut of fish, lately driven in, would leave the coast, in fact there would then be utter destitution.

Revd D. Murphy, parish priest of Kinsale, then stated that action not words or speeches was needed to alleviate destitution, disease and misery after the destruction of the potato crop, 'the staple food of the great bulk of the people'. He proposed to send a deputation to the lord lieutenant, Lord Bessborough, to request funding for the bridge. These works, he pointed out, would 'combine the most extensive employment with the most permanent advantages'.[71]

The deputation that met Lord Bessborough on 12 September 1846 included the Revd D. Murphy, Revd W. Meade, vicar of Kinsale, Mr R. Dunn, representing the barony of Kinsale, and Mr C. Gibbons, representing the rural barony of Courcies. Revd Meade presented their case for a government grant in aid of local taxes for the construction of a bridge across the river Bandon. The advantages of uniting the two baronies by a bridge were outlined. Agriculture, trade and commerce would be enhanced as well as road connectivity between Cork city and the south-west of the county. The deputation informed Lord Bessborough of the great destitution in the locality as a result of the total destruction of the potato crop and the urgent need to provide employment. They impressed on him that the peace of the country was at stake and Mr Gibbons gave an account of the destitution prevalent in Courcies.

> There were 400 families, whose sole daily subsistence was six pounds of Indian meal to each family, issued by the relief committee on labour tickets. Though the smallness of this allowance necessarily produced great privations ... there had not been a single act of theft or outrage committed. When their own supply of provisions was exhausted, the poor people came to the relief committee beseeching that employment should be provided for them. Their words were, give us work or food, we are starving, we are not beasts, we cannot eat grass.

A major cause of concern for the government and those in authority was social unrest leading to riots, outrages and theft. Mr Gibbons pointed out that the 'present' mode of crossing by ferry from Kinsale to Courcies was unsatisfactory, as it prevented the 'speedy transmission of troops from the garrison at Kinsale into the district beyond the river'. Despite the strong case made by the deputation for public money, Lord Bessborough informed them that all the monies had been expended under the March 1846 acts. He encouraged the deputation to make an application for sessions to provide employment under Lord John Russell's act.[72] In other words, the application was a dead letter and an opportunity was lost to provide much needed employment as well as improving infrastructure.

In 1846, there was a drastic decline in potato production due to the effects of the blight in the previous season.[73] The cultivation of potato crops was a labour-intensive activity and the decline in output resulted in high unemployment for agricultural labourers in Kinsale union. However, this was not the only problem as ancillary services provided to the farming community by the sand-boatmen of Kinsale and Innishannon were also affected by the crisis. Before the onset of the Famine around 40 sand-boats 'were accustomed to ply between Kinsale and Innishannon in supplying the farmers of Courcies with sand for manure'. There were about 160 men employed on the sand-boats and each load was worth between 12s. and 14s. The majority of farmers were not buying sand because of financial difficulties and this resulted in unemployment for the sand-boatmen. By the winter of 1846, only five sand-boats employing 20 men were working on the river. Thus, the unemployed boatmen who had no other means of subsistence were facing starvation.

Agricultural labourers and farmers were not the only class affected by the blight as the effects of the calamity extended into the fishing community. The price and market for fish had collapsed. Sprat that sold for £5 in the pre-Famine era was being sold for 30s. and even at the lower price much of the sprat was unsaleable.[74] The lack of money wages in the economy and high unemployment meant that there was little demand for fish. Furthermore, the barter system that existed before the Famine had completely broken down, as fish had been exchanged for potatoes in the countryside. The loss of the potato crop meant that the fishermen on the south coast were as vulnerable to destitution as the farm labourers.

During the winter of 1846 distress was increasing in Kinsale union and employment was urgently required. The reorganization of public works under the Labour Rate act was causing delays as presentment sessions could no longer be called by local landlords. This became the duty of the lord lieutenant of a county and only occurred when the condition of a district became critical.[75]

Eventually, on 5 October 1846, an extraordinary presentments session was held in Kinsale courthouse for the barony of Kinsale. The courthouse was thronged with the unemployed labourers of the town and district. The first presentment under the Labour Rate act was for the bridge across the river Bandon that the deputation from Kinsale presented to Lord Bessborough in

September. The presentment was passed at a cost of £4,400 for the bridge and construction of roads leading to the bridge. The ratepayers of the district – who were willing to tax themselves – were most anxious to have this work executed and hoped that the officers from the Board of Works would reflect the necessity of this project in their report.[76] Another useful project presented for at the sessions was the building of a public quay in Kinsale. This work would give employment to the labourers and masons of the town. The latter were suffering great privations and were employed by the relief committee during the previous season at a rate of 1s. 3d. per day.[77] Although some reproductive works were presented the majority of presentments were for road construction and repairs, which were regarded as the most useful way of providing modest yet extensive employment.[78] Revd Webb welcomed the new Innishannon road presented for at the sessions as the area was under-developed due to the high number of absentee landlords. He affirmed that it would provide much needed employment 'to the exceedingly destitute poor of that district'. However, some roads that cut through private property were not welcomed by self-interested parties. A new line of road that was passed for the barony of Courcies was deemed 'a useless waste of property' by one proprietor at the sessions. In total the amount of presentments granted at the October sessions amounted to around £11,000.[79]

The Labour Rate act was designed to curb the perceived abuses, waste of government money and mismanagement that the government believed had occurred in the previous year; also, the government had never intended public works to promote long term improvements.[80] Hence, the Board of Works rejected the application for the building of a public quay in Kinsale as it was deemed to be outside the auspices of the act. Furthermore, the Labour Rate act was introduced as a temporary measure and was due to expire in August 1847. Consequently, the Board rejected the presentment for the bridge as the works could not be executed within the time-frame of the act. However, the Board of Works did provide extensive employment on road works in Kinsale union but were sometimes hampered by self-interested landowners. In December 1846, public works had to be suspended on the mail-coach road between Kinsale and Cork due to the objections of a landed proprietor.[81]

The conditions of employment for labourers had also changed with the introduction of task work, which was a government initiative to control wages on public works.[82] The policy under Peel's government was a daily wage for labourers on public works, whereas wages were paid for each portion of work completed under the task work system. This change in policy was introduced to reduce the labourers' perceived indolence that had supposedly prevailed during the previous season.[83] The introduction of task work was fiercely resisted by workers and led to distress riots in Kinsale. On 31 October 1846, a number of men refused to work on task-work terms and were discharged from public works. On the following Thursday a group of around 400 men gathered in the town of Kinsale. The labourers had not tasted food during the day and proceeded to visit the bakers' shops where they demanded bread. In order to prevent injury being done to their premises, the owners handed the bread out to the famishing labourers who then left quietly. The clergymen of the district were praised for their efforts and their appeals to prevent violence. In addition, the willingness of the tradespeople to give food to the starving labourers was acclaimed for the salutary effect it had on the people.[84] Riots also broke out in Ballinspittle and a military force was dispatched when labourers refused to work by task and threatened to get food wherever they found it.[85] During the winter of 1846, further disturbances were recorded in Kinsale union, when a haggard of corn worth £200 was destroyed by a malicious fire.[86] By the end of 1846, distress riots in Kinsale union had ceased as survival became the main focus of the labouring population.

In the barony of Courcies the demand for extra employment on public works was unrelenting on a system where demand outstripped supply. On 13 December 1846 a presentments session, under the Labour Rate act, was held in Ballinspittle under the chairmanship of Thomas Cuthbert. A dispute over the numbers of persons employed on roads in the barony arose between the officers of Public Works and the attendees at the meeting. There were 400 men employed on the public works and it was estimated that another 150 men needed employment to prevent death and starvation in the district. Mr Gibbons stated it was desirable that more than one member in a family should be employed. He pointed out that a man earned a maximum of 6s. a week at task work, which would not support a family of eight or ten, whereas under the fixed wages scheme a man was able to earn 8s. 4d. During the first two weeks of December there was a frightful increase in destitution in the barony of Courcies. The price of food had dramatically increased, with Indian meal priced between 2s. 4d. and 2s. 6d. per stone.[87] As labourers became weaker and more debilitated they were less capable of performing enough task work to earn a subsistence wage.[88] Gibbons knew of a man who only earned 5s. a week on task work to support a family of nine. In Gibbon's view more family members needed employment on public works due to the inadequacy in wages, the high cost of provisions and the debilitated state of the workforce. However, Captain Huband, inspecting officer, replied that he could not employ more than one member of a family under the Labour Rate act. He pointed out that there were 30,000 persons employed on road works in West Riding and it would increase to 60,000 if Mr Gibbon's proposal was adopted. Although Captain Huband admitted that he had employed 'two members of a family under special circumstances and strong representations, but in doing so he had, he believed, exceeded his instructions'.[89]

By the end of 1846, 441,000 persons were employed on public works.[90] Initially one of the main concerns of the government was to restrict the numbers employed on public works by introducing impediments, such as task work and limiting employment to the heads of families.[91] Despite the restrictions the numbers employed by the Board of Works was spiralling out of control and any attempt to curb demand was fiercely resisted by the local committees. Furthermore, the abandonment of farming activities by labourers in favour of public works left the cultivation of crops unattended. At the December presentment sessions Revd O'Connor, parish priest of Courcies, said: 'It was a dreadful business to have the whole population of the county employed on roads, while the agriculture of the county was suspended'. Notwithstanding the priest's appeal all the presentments passed were for roads.[92] The neglect of agricultural work was to have a detrimental effect on the amount of seed potatoes planted for the 1847 harvest.

One project that was endorsed by the government was the establishment of four fish-curing stations around the country.[93] Kinsale was named as one of the four stations and a sufficient amount of salt was to be provided for curing at the facility. The *Freeman's Journal* was scathing of the government's aid to the Irish deep sea fisheries and reported that the development of the fisheries could not be done by 'such small and comparatively inefficient aid as the providing of salt to cure the fish'.[94] Many poor fishermen in Kinsale were not equipped with good boats or fishing gear to enable them to catch the quantities of fish required for curing. Thus, the provision of fish-curing facilities was not going to improve the condition of these fishermen.

By January 1847, poverty and destitution had become endemic in Kinsale union. The demand for relief in any form – in food, on public works or in the workhouse – was increasing rapidly. One important concession the government made to the relief committees was permission to provide relief to the poor in the form of soup.[95] As famine conditions intensified causing devastation among the poorer classes, Kinsale relief committee established a bakery in the town, which supplied 1,720 poor inhabitants with bread at a rate of 6d. for a four pound loaf. A soup kitchen was also connected to the bakery where the poor could buy one and a half pints of soup with a quarter pound of bread for ½d. A second soup kitchen was established in Dunderrow, an area that was suffering from great destitution. Despite all the relief efforts, from private charities, public subscriptions and government donations, deaths from starvation were beginning to occur.[96] From the beginning of 1847, the severity of famine in Kinsale town and surrounding districts was beginning to overwhelm the relief services.

A huge burden was placed on Kinsale relief committee as it was estimated that over half the town's population was suffering from destitution. Out of a population of approximately 7,500 there were around 3,000 solely dependent on the fishery and around 1,200 reliant on agriculture and other labour. During the tempestuous winter of 1846 the deep sea fishery had been totally un-remunerative. Thus, a class that was never far removed from poverty sank deeper into destitution. One relief committee member described the state of the fishermen as 'one of the most appalling destitution'. In order to prevent starvation they had pawned their clothes, furniture and fishing gear. The boat owners had advanced those in their employment small sums of money. However, that relief was discontinued due to hardship the boat owners, themselves, were experiencing. Similarly, the labouring population of the town suffered the same privations as those in other localities. Moreover, destitution was not confined to the fishing and labouring populations; artisans of all trades had suffered extreme hardship due to unemployment with many abandoning their trades to work on the roads.[97]

In the winter of 1847 the poor, who had hitherto been reluctant to enter the workhouse, were now flocking to it in great numbers viewing it as their only chance of survival. By February, Kinsale workhouse was completely overcrowded, which led to an increase in death and disease. The workhouse built to accommodate 500 contained 1,050 inmates and the guardians deemed it necessary to refuse any further admissions. As destitution increased throughout Kinsale union, the financial burden compelled the guardians to strike a supplementary rate of 1s. 6d. in the pound 'to enable them to carry on the business of the union a little longer'.[98] The union was almost bankrupt and could not meet the huge demand for relief, which exacerbated the problem for the relief committees and charitable organizations.

Revd Lulem, Catholic curate, and Dr Jago, Kinsale poor law guardian, gave an insight into the living conditions and the effects of famine on the poor of the town. After visiting around 200 houses to issue coal tickets on orders from the relief committee, they gave the following account:

> Only two houses, out of two hundred, in which there was any appearance of food; and in scarcely any was there a particle of fire. And in those houses where a fire was observable, it was in every instance composed of pieces of broken furniture. The poor inhabitants of those huts were virtually in rags, and some of the children were literally naked, whilst misery, destitution and hunger were strongly impressed on them all. Several of them were confined to their beds affected in most instances with fever and diarrhoea; and their household furniture seemed to have been transferred to the pawn-office. A few tattered and filthy rags composed the bed covering of nearly all, whilst the atmosphere of their rooms was tainted with the fated effuvia of the decomposed straw, which was used in every instance as a bed, and which probably had not been renewed for months previous. Few of the poor people had taken any kind of food for twelve hours preceeding; many not for twenty four hours, and some not for the previous thirty nine hours ... deaths have occurred from starvation, and that the constitution of the people at large is becoming gradually undermined from the scantiness of their food, their want of clothing and the absence of fire to impart a ray of warmth to their wretched dwellings.[99]

Similar accounts were given by Revd Webb and Achiles Daunt, poor law guardian, for different districts in the locality. Moreover, the failure of the Board of Works to only sanction £3,753 for works presented at the October sessions was having a detremintal effect on the employment of the labouring poor in the barony of Kinsale. By February 1847, several of the works granted were closed and the remaining works, with over 600 labourers employed, were rapidly coming to an end. Kinsale relief committee urged the Board of Works to sanction some of the reproductive works passed without effect.[100]

The chairman of Kinsale relief committee, John Heard, was directed to write to the under-secretary of state for Ireland, Thomas Redington, to highlight the plight of the poor. He outlined the need for more works to be sanctioned as a large number of labourers were to be discharged from public works and despite the best efforts of the relief committee and the benevolence of the town's inhabitants, distress was acute in Kinsale. Heard pointed out that the workhouse was filled to excess, with several hundred more applicants awaiting admission and every effort to relieve the destitution in the town was being done locally. He stated: 'We can do no more, the people, if not employed, must starve'.[101]

The unrelenting distress caused by famine brought women into public affairs.[102] Gratuitous relief was organized by the Sisters of Mercy in Kinsale. Twice daily, the nuns provided food to the famine-stricken children of Kinsale 'who with few exceptions were actually starving'.[103] In addition, a large number of people also benefited from the free distribution of soup by the nuns. The largest society formed by women was the Ladies' Committee for Ireland and in a number of towns many of these committees helped to raise money and provide food for the distressed people.[104] The Kinsale Ladies' Committee effectively contributed to famine relief with members distributing around 600 quarts of soup each day. Some soup was provided free to the most destitute while some was sold for 1d. per quart.[105]

In the winter of 1846, one of the most important private relief associations formed in response to the crisis was the Central Relief Committee of the Society of Friends – the Quakers. They succeeded in collecting around £200,000 in subscriptions and food from abroad, chiefly from the United States for famine relief in Ireland. The Quakers were to the forefront in establishing soup kitchens but also provided donations to relief committees.[106] On 9 February 1847, William and Joseph Harvey arrived in Kinsale in response to a memorial from the relief committee on behalf of the destitute fishermen. The Harveys met with members of the relief committee and complimented them on the well-ordered and interesting relief operations in place. They were impressed by the bakery and the proposed extension, which would give additional employment as well as meeting the increasing demand for bread. The Harveys reserved their highest praise for Kinsale Ladies' Committee who attended the soup kitchen and 'with their own hands distribute a considerable quantity each day' to the poor.[107] The work ethic of the women in Kinsale was commendable, as in Victorian times many women involved in charitable organizations did not afford personal labour, fearing that visiting the hovels of the poor was 'too shocking for female delicacy to sustain'.[108] Individual efforts were also a feature of famine relief in Kinsale. Major Deeds and the officers of the 35th depot stationed at Charles Fort opened a soup kitchen in the village of Summercove where they provided around 80 persons with gratuitous food daily. Overall, the Harveys were satisfied with the public and private relief operations in Kinsale, which provided outdoor relief to around 1,800 persons. However, the object of their journey was to assess the state of the fishermen. They accompanied some members of the Ladies' Committee who were on their way to supply tickets to the families of the fishermen. Even though the fishermen were slightly better-off than when the application was made to the Quakers in mid-January, they were still in a state of destitution. One of the ladies explained to them that most of the families existed on one meal every 24 hours and their clothes were in the pawn shops. Furthermore, the fishermen were obliged to go to sea, sometimes for days together, without sufficient clothing to shield them from the inclement weather. She illustrated the painful privations that occurred from exhaustion by the following example:

> A poor man belonging to one of the hookers, returning from a fishing cruise of a day or two, was so reduced by want of nourishment and cold, that the slapping or shifting of a sail, after entering the harbour, was sufficient to throw him overboard, when, being too feeble to struggle, he sunk and was drowned.

The cause of such misery was directly related to the failure of the potato crop. Each fisherman required a double supply of food before going to sea, one for his own support and another portion for his family. When potatoes were plentiful this was achievable but when the potato crop failed and other provisions became expensive, the fishermen and their families 'sunk into indigence'. During the winter of 1846–7 the Kinsale fishery was very unproductive, due to the severe weather, scarcity of fish and the inability of people to purchase the little amount of fish caught. Another cause of the fishermen's destitution was their indebtedness to the Loan Fund and as the loans became due they were forced to pawn their belongings to meet the demands of the bank. Employment on public works was unattainable, as the fishermen were 'quite unfit for any labour but fishing'. Many sought refuge in the workhouse and many more were 'proper objects for it'. However, the workhouse was overcrowded and closed to admissions and outdoor relief was their only hope of survival. Although destitution was rife in Kinsale's fishing community, the Harveys believed 'but for the activity and benevolent care of the Ladies' Committee ... it is probable that many might have perished altogether'. To this end they left a sum of money for the fishermen's relief with the Ladies' Committee.[109]

In Kinsale town, the role of the relief committee and private charitable organizations in providing outdoor relief prevented many deaths from starvation. However, the rural areas within Kinsale union were not as fortunate. At the end of January 1847, the parish priest of Tracton, Revd Corkran, wrote a letter pleading for aid to 'friends in England'. Revd Corkran was a member of the Ballyfeard relief committee and he appealed for funds to keep the two soup kitchens they had established in the district open. He described the condition of his parishioners as follows:

> Ballyfeard comprises a territory of three miles radius (ever remarkable for the cultivation of potatoes,) it contains 1,200 destitute subjects for relief, each on average having five in family. Of these 700 are employed on the public works, earning from 4s. to 6s. per week, and paying 2s. 9d. per stone for Indian corn flour. Life thus sustained is but a protracted death. The destitute *unemployed* on the public works are in a state of appalling misery, which I will not, because I could not, describe. They are to my own knowledge frequently without tasting any food for 48 hours, and then glad to get raw turnips, cabbage, or sea-weed, which they greedily devour. Some sustain life by visiting in troops the houses of the gentry, some by casual charity, some by plunder. Our Union workhouse is full. The weekly average of deaths in my parishes, from slow starvation, is four; three such cases occurred this day.[110]

The second potato crop failure had a devastating effect on the rural population in Kinsale union. In the rural parishes, there was no network of private charities to provide relief for the destitute. Local relief committees were dependent on dwindling subscriptions and employment on the public works had failed in preventing deaths from starvation.

In the second year of distress, the temporary relief measures introduced by the Whig government had failed to halt the crisis. A policy of non-interference in the food trade combined with a refusal to provide relief in the form of food for the destitute was a major mistake. The second potato crop failure had cataclysmic consequences for the population of Kinsale union as public works failed to provide a subsistence wage. The restrictive policies pursued by the government contrasted sharply with the contribution of charitable organizations and individuals to famine relief. The provision of food to the destitute undoubtedly saved lives in the winter of 1846–7. The government belatedly recognized the benefits of soup kitchens. As deaths from starvation and disease were increasing a new system of temporary relief – soup kitchens – was put in place by the government to try and halt the Famine's deadly progress.

DEATH AND DISEASE

Between 1841 and 1851 the population of Kinsale Union declined from 41,014 to 30,051, or by around 27 per cent.[111] This change in the demographic caused by emigration and mortality can be attributed to the Great Famine. The appearance of potato blight that resulted in repeated crop failures caused suffering and distress to the poorer classes of society – vagrants, beggars, cottiers and the labouring classes – 'whose means would not enable them to obtain grain food as a substitute for their ordinary diet'.[112] The consequences of this calamity were deaths from starvation and dietary deficiency diseases such as scurvy and pellagra that accounted for some mortality, but the vast majority of deaths resulted from a range of infectious diseases. During the Famine period, these epidemics were facilitated by the impairment of a person's immune system from starvation and the loss of resistance to disease in the general population. Among the contributory factors that helped spread these diseases were increased vagrancy, mendicancy and mobility, with people searching for food, neglect of personal and domestic hygiene, and the overcrowding of public institutions. Diseases such as typhus fever, relapsing fever, dysentery, diarrhoea, tuberculosis, measles and smallpox that were always endemic in the lower classes were magnified during the Famine.[113] The reappearance of Asiatic cholera in 1848–9 – although not one of the diseases of the Great Famine – dramatically increased suffering and mortality in Kinsale union.

A correlation existed between prolonged shortages of food and epidemic diseases and by the winter of 1846–7 large-scale starvation followed by numerous infectious diseases was evident in Kinsale. The potato crop failure was harshest on the labouring classes and even for tradesmen that could afford to purchase food the loss of the potato resulted in 'scurvy or purpura'.[114] The health of the poor was also impacted by the use of raw or badly cooked food, but it was the scarcity of food that resulted in deaths from starvation.

By the beginning of 1847, reports of deaths from starvation were beginning to emerge from Kinsale. The town that had hitherto been considered fortunate having escaped the worst ravages of the calamity was 'plunged in as deep misery, and has as dreary a prospect before it, as any other part of this extensive country'. Despite all the efforts of the relief committee and charitable organizations, deaths from starvation were becoming 'matters of frequent occurrence' in the locality.[115] During the winter of 1846–7 the shortage of food and its price became critical in Kinsale. As the poor faced a third year of distress with many living on one meal a day, or less, it was inevitable that deaths would occur.

On 28 January 1847, Paul Mullin, a labourer from Brown's Mills, near Kinsale, died from exhaustion 'caused by want of food'. The man had been working on the public roads when he collapsed and died. Dr Robert Warren, medical officer of Kinsale union, described in detail the signs of famine cachexia or lingering starvation when he gave evidence to the inquest on the man's death:

He found the body lying in a small hut, on the side of the road; found the whole body much emaciated, the eyes sunken, the abdomen also sunken; on opening the cavity of the abdomen found the intestines perfectly free from fatty matter, the gall bladder greatly distended with bile, the stomach devoid of solid food, but containing about a wine glass of fluid; the small intestines also empty, as well as the large with the exception of the colon, which contained faeces, the result of a small quantity of food taken at least four and twenty hours before his death.[116]

Revd D. Murphy, parish priest of Kinsale, reported that Mullin's death was 'only one of numerous cases of a like nature' and 'the already satieted graveyards bear melancholy evidence to the ravages of starvation in this parish'. Revd Murphy highlighted the plight of one class in particular, the fishermen and their dependants who accounted for almost half of Kinsale's population, and who were in 'a state of destitution beyond the power of human tongue to describe'. He described members of his flock as 'starving creatures ... worn, emaciated and feeble' and in 'whose skeletal faces' he could scarcely recognize a single feature.[117] In the parish of Tracton there was an average of four deaths weekly from starvation and similar accounts were reported throughout the union.[118]

Although many deaths from famine-induced starvation occurred it was epidemic diseases that invariably follow famine that increased the misery, suffering and mortality in the country. The consequences of famine for any considerable duration was an outbreak of 'famine fever'. This term encompassed two types of fever, typhus and relapsing fever, even though in the mid-1840s the agent of fever was unknown. The vector for both types of fever was the body louse. A bacterial organism, *Rickettsia*, caused typhus and a spirochaete species was the causative organism for relapsing fever with the disease being transferred from person to person.[119] The increase in famine fever was generally associated with food shortages that compelled people to leave their homes and seek refuge in towns and cities. In January 1847, a petition from the town of Kinsale was presented to parliament, stating that 'the system of electoral divisions under the Irish poor law had acted oppressively in forcing the worn-out poor to go from the rural districts to the towns'.[120] This migration of the poor into the town provided ideal conditions for the transfer of contagious diseases, as people – some already carriers of disease – gathered together in unhealthy and unhygienic conditions.

One of the distinguishing features between both fevers was the susceptibility of the upper classes to develop typhus fever, whereas relapsing fever was more prevalent in the lower classes. In Innishannon, mortality due to typhus fever was 16 times greater among the higher and middle classes than among the poor.[121] The lower rate of typhus mortality among the poor may be attributed to the immunity they developed over time to the disease.[122] During the Famine, fever combined with dysentery and diarrohea proved fatal in many cases.[123] Bacillary dysentery was also known as the 'bloody flux' and was a highly contagious disease caused by bacilli micro-organisms and spread by contaminated water, flies and human contact.[124] Painful bowel discharges and severe diarrhoea with passage of blood were some of the symptoms of famine dysentery.

In early March 1846, a committee appointed by the government published a report which confirmed that fever and other epidemic diseases were increasing throughout the country. The medical officer from Ballinspittle who responded to the committee's inquiries emphasized the increase in fever and diarrhoea in the area, and he attributed this to the consumption of diseased potatoes. He further noted the contagious nature of the disease as the dreaded fever passed 'through the whole family, if once admitted'. In addition, Dr Bishop, medical officer at Kinsale fever hospital, reported that fever was widespread during the previous eight months and commented on the lack of employment in the area and the scarcity and unsoundness of food as probable causes of the epidemic.[125] Many medical officers were concerned about the inadequate medical facilities available to deal with the impending crisis.[126]

On 24 March 1846, the government responded to the committee's report by enacting a Temporary Fever act, to provide for the treatment of fever and other epidemic diseases among the poor. Five unpaid commissioners were appointed by the government to a Central Board of Health, who were to advise and direct boards of guardians on the provision of fever hospitals and dispensaries in their unions. Under the poor law, the guardians had three options for dealing with fever patients; first they could rent a house for the treatment of patients, secondly they could erect a building or thirdly they could remove patients to a fever hospital, the cost of removal and maintenance being chargeable to the rates.[127] In December 1845, the poor law commissioners recommended that Kinsale board of guardians should build a fever hospital, as all fever cases were admitted into the general workhouse hospital. However, the guardians resisted any demands to build a fever hospital as they deemed it an unnecessary expense due to the existence of one in the area. By February 1846 the prevalence of fever in the workhouse forced the guardians to enter into an arrangement with the manager of the fever hospital for the removal of all fever cases from the workhouse. A month after the arrangement was in place the workhouse finance committee paid £12 8s. 8d. for treatment of paupers in the fever hospital.[128]

The guardians did, however, realize the deficiencies in the system provided by the medical charities and in particular the issue of governance and funding for hospitals and dispensaries. At their weekly meeting on 5 February 1846 they put forward suggestions for reform of the medical charities. The guardians recommended a compulsory rate to be raised at the same time as the poor rate and that fever hospitals and dispensaries should be governed and managed by boards of guardians, thus removing the voluntary funding and patronage associated with the medical charities.[129] Despite the guardians' acknowledgment of the shortcomings in the provisions of medical relief for the sick poor, they steadfastly refused to build a fever hospital. By May 1846, only three unions in County Cork – Fermoy, Mallow and Kinsale – had not put in place any measures for the construction of a separate fever hospital.[130] As disease became more prevalent the accommodation and equipment in the fever hospital and dispensaries proved totally insufficient to meet the unfolding crisis.

By the winter of 1846–7, famine conditions in the barony of Courcies had exacerbated the proliferation of disease. Dr Elmore, Ballinspittle, reported that disease was spreading throughout the locality and was 'brought on by want of food, fire and clothing'.[131] Similar accounts were given on the prevalence of fever and diarrhoea in Kinsale.[132] As infectious diseases were rapidly increasing the medical officers were overwhelmed by their scale and severity. The inadequacy of Kinsale fever hospital to deal with the crisis was highlighted at the presentments session in October 1846. To this end, a presentment of £200 was granted as the hospital was in 'such a state' that patients' lives were at risk. Dr Bishop stated:

> The accommodation was most fearful. There were two convalescent patients in a bed, a state of things which should not be tolerated.[133]

By the beginning of January 1847, Kinsale workhouse and the additional accommodation provided at the old jail became overcrowded due to the large number of admissions. This became a major factor in generating disease. In the workhouse there were around 900 inmates and the medical officer feared the impossibility of separating all the sick from the healthy. Moreover, the majority of inmates in the old jail were children and the medical officer reported on the unhealthy aspect of confinement in the ward, with many of the children suffering from 'the prevailing epidemic' – fever.[134] From October 1846 the admission rates to Kinsale workhouse escalated reaching a crisis point in January 1847, which contributed to a high death rate in the subsequent months. Table 3 indicates the developing crisis in Kinsale over the winter and spring of 1846–7.[135]

In response to the reports of disease and death sweeping the country, the Board of Health that had been disbanded in August 1846 was reappointed by the lord lieutenant in February 1847.[136] It was obvious by then that the provision of medical services for the famine-stricken population was at breaking point. To this end, one of the recommendations proposed by the Board of Health was the establishment of temporary fever hospitals and dispensaries, which required the amendment of the Temporary Fever act in April 1847. The Board of Health retained overall control of the emergency hospitals and dispensaries, but local responsibility was transferred from the boards of guardians to the local relief committees who were responsible for all costs associated with the facilities, including doctors' salaries. The Board received 576 applications of which 373 were granted, which indicated the inadequacies in

Table 3. Number of admissions to Kinsale workhouse and number and percentage of deaths recorded from October 1846 to July 1847[137]

1846–7	Number of admissions	Number of deaths	Proportion of deaths to admissions
October	323	9	3%
November	280	19	7%
December	355	27	8%
January	542	12	2%
February	489	50	10%
March	538	99	18%
April	470	82	17%
May	494	113	23%
June	320	76	24%
July	237	48	20%

the existing system and the level of distress in the country.[138] During May and June, two temporary hospitals were granted for Kinsale union as well as medical appliances and requisites for Kinsale hospital. The Ballinspittle emergency hospital covered the distressed barony of Courcies and the Huddersfield hospital covered the electoral divisions of Carrigaline, Liscleary and Templebredy.[139] These emergency measures that the Board of Health implemented proved effective in halting the epidemic. On 16 September 1847, at the Kinsale board of guardians' weekly board meeting, the medical officer reported on the cessation of fever in the area, thereby enabling him to move infirm patients into the fever sheds.[140]

In August 1847, all the temporary measures introduced by the government for relieving distress were transferred to the poor law.[141] This made the provision of medical relief a local issue. In Kinsale union the relief committees signalled their intention to close their hospitals without delay. This placed a huge financial and medical burden on an almost insolvent union. On 14 October 1847, the balance of funds in the union's accounts was only £125 4s. 11d. The guardians' funds were so stretched they proposed to rent Kinsale fever hospital on a yearly basis for the use of fever patients in the entire union, but were directed by the commissioners to take over the hospital from the relief committee. The provision of healthcare for inmates in the workhouse became chaotic. In November the Board of Health issued the guardians with a warning about accepting fever and dysentery cases into the workhouse hospital. The guardians strenuously denied this allegation – made by a local doctor – and replied that all cases were sent to the fever hospital. However, they stated: 'There was no longer any necessity for separate establishments in consequence of the almost total absence of fever in that part of the country'. Thus, infectious patients were not separated from general hospital patients, leading to a continuous level of contagion in the workhouse, which resulted in unnecessary suffering and mortality. By February 1848, both Carrigaline and Ballinspittle fever hospitals were closed down. Immediately after the closure a report that malignant fever was on the increase in Courcies was forwarded to the Board of Health. Again the guardians denied the prevalence of fever in the district.[142] Although fever had diminished in the union, it had not disappeared. The closure of the emergency hospitals and the disregard for the directives from the Board of Health meant that infectious diseases persisted in Kinsale union.

The rate of mortality was also a concern for the Board of Health and to ascertain the causes of the high death rate they issued a circular to doctors around the country. The replies identified the proportion of typhus and relapsing fever in certain localities.[143] On 16 October 1847, Dr Courtenay, Nohoval, reported:

> The type of fever here is the simple continued, and a few cases of exclusive typhus; the usual duration is from five to eleven days with a peculiar tendency to repeated relapses – out of 250 cases, 240 relapsed'.[144]

The type of fever identified by Dr Courtenay was relapsing fever, which was prevalent throughout the Famine years in Kinsale union. Patient records from Kinsale workhouse also indicate a high incidence of fever. From July 1849 to July 1850, there were over 544 patients admitted to Kinsale fever hospital, with workhouse paupers accounting for around 70 per cent of admissions. Fever accounted for around 97 per cent of the diseases and dysentery, small-pox, measles, apoplexy, lung inflamation, dropsy and protuberance were among the other diseases listed. The average length of stay in the fever hospital was 26 days and the split between male and female admissions was almost equal. The vulnerbility of the young to infectious diseases in Kinsale workhouse was highlighted with around 40 per cent of admissions aged 15 years and younger. These children mainly suffered from fever and diseases such as dysentery, measles and small-pox were also recorded, the latter proving fatal in many cases.[145]

In March 1849, the high mortality in Kinsale workhouse prompted Mr French, a member of parliament, to comment: 'the arrangement made for the care of patients in Kinsale, Carlow, Parsonstown, Nenagh and other unions, showed that the poor law was most negligently and ill-administered'.[146] Over the Famine period, Kinsale workhouse earned a reputation as a place of pestilence and disease, which resulted in a high mortality rate as outlined in table 4.

During the summer of 1849 the death rate in Kinsale workhouse spiralled and the major contributory factor to mortality was cholera. Once cholera appeared in Britain its arrival in Ireland was inevitable. To this end, the Central Board of Health issued a circular on 1 September 1848 to the guardians of each poor law union, advising on measures to be taken in advance of its arrival. The disease spread fear among the population. A sudden onset of diarrhoea usually

Table 4. Record of deaths in Kinsale workhouse from January 1846 to December 1852[147]

Year	Number of deaths
1846	92
1847	569
1848	283
1849	1,230
1850	169
1851	151
1852	132
Total	**2,626**

accompanied by vomiting resulting in severe dehydration proved fatal in many cases. This highly contagious disease is caused by the bacterium *Vibrio cholerae* and is spread by contaminated water and food.[148] In 1849, the means of transmission had not been discovered and there was divided opinion as to whether or not cholera was contagious.[149] The opinion of the Board of Health was that 'contagion has little, if any, influence in its propagation'. As a consequence of their misguided opinion they recommended that seperating the sick from the healthy was not required. The circular outlined that the best course of action was to treat cholera patients in their own homes. According to the Board, delays in removing a patient to hospital could result in loss of life due to the shortness in duration of the attack and the sudden onset of the disease. Hence, there was no need for an extended system of hospital accommodation but an efficient and prompt system of dispensary relief was recommended.[150]

On 25 January 1849, the circular from the Board of Health was read at the weekly meeting of the Kinsale board of guardians. A resolution was passed to furnish and fit out two wards at the dispensary house in Barrack Street, Kinsale for the reception of cholera cases. The Kinsale dispensary physician was authorized to treat any cases that might arise and also to employ nurses and other attendants as deemed necessary, but until the arrival of cholera patients the wards were to be used as auxillaries to the fever hospital. The clerk was directed to inform the dispensary physicians that notification to the Board was required when the first cholera outbreak occurred in Kinsale union.

By April, Kinsale board of guardians had followed the circular from the Board of Health and the necessary preparations were in place to deal with the impending pandemic. In accordance with the guidelines they authorized the dispensary physicians to take charge of any cholera cases in their districts and the union would bear the financial costs for any medicine and dietary requirements the patients required. In addition, the dispensary physicians were supplied with four pairs of blankets, two bed ticks and two pairs of sheets. Additional expenses were also incurred by the union with the procurement of coffins and biers 'with a view to the speedy interment of the sufferers', and the dispensary doctors were allocated funds for funeral expenses.

The Board of Health also called the guardians attention to the Nuisance Removal and Disease Prevention act, which made them responsible for general cleanliness and the removal of nuisances within the union.[151] All the costs associated with the cholera epidemic were paid out of the poor rates.[152] The high rates of pay offered to those administering to cholera patients significantly contributed to costs. The cholera physicians and apothecary received five guineas and three guineas a week respectively, and the cholera nurse received 5s. a week, which was double her normal wage. Revd Lulem, Roman Catholic chaplain, who attended to the religious needs of the patients, received two guineas a week. This placed a huge financial burden on the ratepayers of Kinsale union. On 19 April, the clerk was directed to write to the poor law commissioners requesting them to defer the repayment on the government loan until after the harvest 'as destitution is rapidly increasing and the cholera is in our neighbourhood'.[153]

On 3 May 1849 the guardians were notified that cholera had arrived in Kinsale and they immediately directed the house committee to procure extra accommodation for cholera patients. The house committee recommended renting additional buildings at the old jail and dock yard adjoining the auxiliary workhouses. The buildings were rented at a rate of £4 per year for the former and £20 per year for the latter. A burial ground at Clontead, near Belgooly, was also rented at a rate of £5 per year for the interment of cholera victims.[154]

On 22 May 1849 the *Cork Constitution* reported that the cholera had broken out to a fearful extent during the previous week in Kinsale. Captain Brandling, poor law inspector, visited the town and stated that it was 'pitiful to witness scenes there of the dead and dying'. Although extra doctors were employed and the services of the Sisters of Mercy were accepted to tend to the patients in the workhouse, the number of cholera cases was increasing. This caused alarm among the general population. Up to noon on 21 May, the total number of cases was 596 of which 287 had died, 130 had recovered and a further 179 remained under treatment.[155]

The scale and severity of the cholera outbreak in Kinsale had overwhelmed the medical officers and attendants. Although the dispensary house was designated a cholera hospital, the additional accommodation required for the influx of paupers was not isolated from the workhouse accommodation. Thus, contagion spread through the workhouse as the sick and the healthy were confined in overcrowded and unsanitary conditions. It was clear to the guardians that the association of cholera patients with others in the workhouse was leading to the spread of the disease. When Dr Elmore, dispensary physician from Courcies, enquired about opening a hospital to accommodate his cholera patients, the guardians severely admonished him. They directed him to treat the cholera sufferers in their own houses, which was the procedure for all the other physicians in the union.[156]

By the end of May as the deaths from cholera increased there was widespread fear of the bodies of those who had died.[157] This was highlighted in a letter to the *Cork Examiner* as the guardians were bitterly criticized over the burial of cholera victims at Clontead cemetery. The panic and fear of the people was expressed as follows:

> No fewer than eighty-five human beings were consigned to their last and only resting place, in a monster pit, dug in a cemetery called Clontead, some two miles distant from Kinsale, and by order of the guardians. A word now as to the effect created by this indecent, inhuman, if not illegal order, of this seemingly irresponsible board. The route which they had to travel to arrive at this pit ... passes through a very populous hamlet called Brown's Mills; and the consequence of this sapient act of theirs was, that they threw the people into the utmost alarm and excitement; and as it is now an established fact, that fright is a predisposing inducement to cholera ... the hamlet referred to above is more prolific in mortality than any place of its extent in this desolate and afflicted county.

In Kinsale, the fear of dying from cholera was parallel to the fear of dying in the workhouse, and justifiably so. An observation as to why those who needed assistance refused to enter the workhouse was made: 'They prefer the miserable uncertainty of relief outside to the awful certainty of death inside'. The workhouse was 'filled to suffocation' and as out-door relief ceased in August 1847 there was no other form of relief available to the destitute.[158] The high mortality in the over-crowded, disease-ridden workhouse was a deterrent to the people for whom it was designed.

The cholera crisis was so extensive that it required three medical officers to attend patients in the town. In addition, Captain Brandling was appointed inspector of cholera cases in Kinsale union. Dr Jago, who had resigned as poor law guardian to take up a position as cholera doctor, reported to the Board on 31 May 1849 that cholera was on the decrease in the union and as a result that no further cholera cases should be admitted to the cholera hospital, unless under a provisional order from a relieving officer. On 14 June, just six weeks after the initial outbreak of cholera, the guardians deemed 'the cholera epidemic has ceased in both town and neighbourhood and the workhouse and auxiliaries are now free from cholera'. They resolved to dismantle the Barrack Street hospital immediately and remove recovering patients to the workhouse hospital. This reduction in medical services was a cost-saving device for the union as reduction in wages and dismissal of staff ensued.[159]

By the end of the epidemic, on 23 June 1849, there were 447 deaths out of 825 cases in Kinsale.[160] Over the course of the following months many more cholera patients were admitted into Kinsale hospital. The disease had a devestating effect on the population of Kinsale, as one observer stated:

The wholesale mortality, occuring at present in this ill-starred union, bids fair to throw far in the shade the charnel reputation which the Skibbereen and Bantry unions attained, in those deplorable years '46 and '47.[161]

During the Famine era, starvation accounted for some mortality but it was the scurge of infectious diseases that gripped the weakened, famine-ridden population that caused the most deaths in Kinsale union. The fearful toll of mortality in Kinsale workhouse was chiefly attributed to contagion that spread through the workhouse unabated. The medical officers were unable and ill-equipped to stem the tide of these contagious diseases that left a trail of death and destruction behind them.

3. Kinsale workhouse

Shelter, food, clothing, medical aid and spiritual consolation, are duly prepared for all persons who enter the workhouse.[1]

The 1838 poor law provided for the establishment of workhouses across the country. An English architect, George Wilkinson, was given the task of designing and supervising the construction of the 130 workhouses, which were built to a standard design with a total capacity of around 94,000. Although the workhouses were hastily built on a stringent budget they were generally structurally sound.[2] Kinsale workhouse was located on a six-acre site in the townland of Rathbeg about a mile outside the town. The administrative block of the workhouse is still used by Cork County Council today, which is a testament to the durability of the building.

Kinsale workhouse was medium sized and capable of accommodating 500 persons. The workhouse was surrounded by high walls and consisted of a complex of buildings, which contained separate accommodation for males and females, an infirmary and idiot wards, exercise yards, kitchen, washroom and storeroom. A chapel, dining hall and school rooms were also included. There was an administrative unit at the front of the building where the boardroom and clerk's office were located and a large hall where paupers were admitted on receipt of an application or ticket provided by a relieving officer for each district.

The workhouse afforded a very low standard of comfort with un-plastered walls and clay or mortar ground floors. Sanitation was poor with privies located near cesspools, which frequently overflowed.[3] It was not surprising that the workhouses had numerous problems with fixture and fittings, ranging from poorly fitted windows and leaking roofs to inadequate drainage and ventilation issues. The meagre facilities inside the buildings and the harsh exteriors were designed to ensure that only persons suffering acute deprivations would seek entry.[4]

Workhouse life was highly regulated and applicants were forced to submit to an oppressive monotony of institutional routine.[5] Paupers were washed, clothed in a workhouse uniform and classified on admission.[6] Applicants for relief included the aged and infirm, the sick and diseased, vagrants and able-bodied destitute, deserted wives and children, orphans, unmarried mothers, prostitutes, and families who became destitute.[7] On admission, families were broken up with men separated from women, children from adults and the sick from the healthy. Idleness was not tolerated in the workhouse and a strict regime of work was enforced, except for the sick or disabled. Work was of a menial nature such as breaking stones for the men and domestic duties for the women. Children were required to attend school and to perform physical tasks around the workhouse after school.[8]

The enforcement of rules and regulations depended on competent and responsible staff and these were appointed by the poor law guardians who were entrusted with the administration of the union. The workhouse was managed by officers under the supervision of a workhouse master. Subordinate officers included a matron who was responsible for the female section of the workhouse, a storeman who was responsible for purchasing food, clothing and other provisions, and medical officers who were responsible for the health of inmates. Minor officials and inmates assisted in duties such as domestic and hospital work.[9]

The administration of Kinsale union was the responsibility of a 28-member board of guardians. In practice, however, the governance of Kinsale workhouse and the administration of the union were carried out by a core group of conscientious individuals who were interested in the fair administration of the poor law. During the Famine years, Kinsale board of guardians met at the workhouse boardroom every Thursday, under the chairmanship of William Meade. Between 2 September 1847 and 16 January 1851, an average attendance of around 10 guardians was recorded, with W. Meade, A. Daunt, Dr Jago, Dr Daunt, T. Knolles, J. Walton and G. Dunn regularly attending meetings.[10] Most of the guardians' time was spent on dealing with financial matters, such as the striking and collecting of rates and supervising the poor rate valuation survey for the union. In addition, the guardians made the final decision on the admission and discharge of paupers and were involved in all aspects of pauper care as outlined in the legislation.[11]

DIET

One of the criteria set out in the poor law was that any inmate should not be afforded better care than that available to the poorest labourer outside the workhouse, and this included diet.[12] To this end, the poor law commissioners laid down guidelines for the minimum food allowances for inmates in a diet designed to be dull and frugal. In general adults were allowed two meals a day to consist of a combination of oatmeal, potatoes and milk. The commissioners recommended that children should be allowed three meals daily and proportionally less than the adults, with bread for supper.[13] The workhouse dietaries were drawn up by the local board of guardians with economy in mind. On 20 November 1841 the following dietary was adopted by the Kinsale board of guardians:

Kinsale workhouse

	Able-bodied males	Able-bodied females
Breakfast	3½ lbs. potatoes	3 lbs. potatoes
	7 oz. oatmeal stirabout	6 oz. oatmeal stirabout
	½ pint milk	½ pint milk
Dinner	4 lbs. potatoes	3½ lbs. potatoes
	1 pint milk	1 pint milk

Children under nine years were to be dieted at the guardians' discretion and children between 9 and 14 years were afforded a similar diet to the able-bodied females. The infirm, sickly and bed-ridden were to be dieted at the discretion of the medical officer.[14] The importance of potatoes as a cheap and nutritious food source is reflected in the pre-Famine diet of the poor in Kinsale workhouse.

By the summer of 1846 potatoes had completely disappeared from the workhouse diet in Kinsale union. As a result the poor law commissioners were asked to recommend a dietary supplement instead of potatoes. The guardians opted for Indian meal as it was a cheap and available food source. The Relief Commission issued instructions on various ways of using Indian corn for human consumption. Among the recipes recommended was suppawn or porridge, which involved the addition of Indian meal to boiling water, milk or broth and was supposed to provide a nutritious meal for adults and children as well as a palliative for bad digestion.[15] Other recipes included various types of breads and puddings and Indian meal became the staple in Kinsale workhouse for the remainder of the Famine. A list of provisions ordered for each week and the cost of a pauper in Kinsale workhouse gives an insight into the changing diet and the frugality of sustenance over the Famine period, outlined in table 5.

Once the potato blight struck and the number of admissions increased, the main concern for the guardians was the cost of the workhouse dietary rather than the nutritional quality of the food. The only departure permitted from an inmate's monotonous diet was for sick inmates as recommended by the Board of Health. This included extra portions of bread, beef or mutton broth and extras such as wine, whiskey and porter.[16] In June 1848 a suspicion prevailed among the guardians that more inmates were receiving a superior diet than were entitled to it. At their weekly meeting on 8 June, the guardians demanded a return on the number of paupers receiving 'an extraordinary diet beyond that of the usual house diet' and a detailed account of the proportion of white bread orders for each pauper. Furthermore, they required the returns to be authenticated by the signature of the medical officer to ensure that the dietary rules were being obeyed.[17]

At the end of August 1850, potatoes were re-introduced to the workhouse dietary. However, after a four-week period these orders were discontinued as Indian meal was a cheaper option at just over £7 per ton.[18] By the winter of 1850 the poor law commissioners were seriously concerned that dietary guidelines were not being followed in Kinsale workhouse and requested a copy of the dietary from the guardians, who responded that the sanitary state of the workhouse and 'the comfortable appearance of the inmates' were 'best proof of the sufficiency of the present dietary'.[19] From 19 October 1850 to 11 January 1851 the average cost of a pauper had been reduced to 9½d. a week, around half of what it had been at the beginning of March 1846.[20]

Table 5. Workhouse weekly orders and cost of a pauper, 1846–1850[21]

5 March 1846	2 September 1847	1 June 1848	26 April 1849	30 May 1850
400 lbs. bread	½ ton Indian meal	2 ton seconds flour	3 ton seconds flour	1 ton seconds flour
700 quarts milk	700 quarts milk	5,000 quarts milk	5,000 quarts milk	3,700 quarts milk
40 lbs. meat	100 lbs. candles	112 lbs. meat	112 lbs. meat	130 lbs. meat
302 weights potatoes	1 cwt. soap	2 ton wholemeal	3 ton wholemeal 6 lb. pepper	1½ ton wholemeal
84 lbs. soap		5 cwt. soap	2 ton Indian meal 2½ cwt. oatmeal	1 ton Indian corn
1 cwt. salt		1 dozen wine	5 cwt. salt	2 cwt. salt
3 bottles wine			12 lbs. tea	2½ lbs. tea
			1 dozen wine 20 lbs. arrow root	½ gal. whiskey
			100 pints porter	26 pints porter
			56 lbs. sugar	21 lbs. sugar
			2 lbs. coffee	1½ lbs. coffee
			½ gal. whiskey	9 lbs. candles
			28 lbs. malt	14 lbs. malt
Cost of pauper 1s. 7d.	Cost of pauper 1s. 5d.	Cost of pauper 1s. 2¾d.	Cost of pauper 1s. 0¼d.	Cost of pauper 9⅗d.

ACCOMMODATION

Before the Great Famine the workhouses were rarely half full, but as destitution increased the demands being made for admission to workhouses was unprecedented.[22] The accommodation crisis for Kinsale workhouse began in January 1847 and as an interim measure the guardians' rented additional accommodation. The old jail on Cork Street was used to accommodate around 200 persons as widespread famine swept the country. The old jail or Desmond Castle was built as a customs house by the earl of Desmond c.1500 and was used as a prison during the 18th century, hence the name assigned to it in the minute books. The crisis in early 1847 highlighted the need for more workhouse accommodation and the inadequacy of the poor law to relieve severe distress. However, this did not deter the government from making the poor law the main vehicle for famine relief from August 1847 onwards.

The 1847 poor law extension act facilitated the transfer of relief to the poor law unions and brought Kinsale workhouse to the forefront of relief measures for the remainder of the Great Famine. The temporary relief measures designed to cope with extraordinary circumstances ceased and all famine relief was then vested in and paid for by each poor law union. One of the provisions of the 1838 poor law legislation was that all relief had to be administered inside the workhouse and outdoor relief was explicitly forbidden.[23] The amendment to the original legislation enabled boards of guardians to give relief outside the workhouse to anyone unable to work due to sickness, disability or age, widows with two or more legitimate children, and orphans. The onus was on poor law guardians to relieve all destitute persons in their locality either inside or outside the workhouse and the ratepayers became financially responsible for poverty in their union.[24]

A significant and draconian measure introduced under the poor law extension act was the Gregory clause, which barred relief to any person holding more than a quarter-acre of land.[25] The intention of this clause was to prevent abuse of public relief and encourage the consolidation of land.[26] In reality it deprived many destitute persons from obtaining relief causing even more suffering and misery. From 1838 to 1847 the poor law was administered from England with a number of assistant commissioners in Ireland. However, changes to the poor law provided for a separate authority in Ireland with each union centrally controlled by a board of poor law commissioners in Dublin.[27] Thus the poor law extension act signalled the British government's decision to make all future famine relief a local and national affair rather than an imperial issue.

Although there was a provision for outdoor relief to be provided in special circumstances under the amended legislation, the commissioners' preferred option was the extension of workhouse accommodation. This view was expressed in their annual report:

> A very important feature in the administration of relief during the present season is the large extent of additional workhouse accommodation provided by the boards of guardians throughout the country. This has taken place under the influence of a strong and growing conviction that the abuses incidental to out-door relief are not to be contended with by any administrative agency, when such relief is conducted on a large scale; and that a system of workhouse relief is preferable, not alone in ordinary times, but in seasons of the severest distress.

In the autumn of 1847, Kinsale was one of 25 unions in the country not to afford outdoor relief under the poor law extension act and all applicants were subject to a test of destitution.[28] Kinsale board of guardians believed that the workhouse could cope with the likely number of admissions as sheds had been erected on the workhouse grounds, which were capable of accommodating 200 inmates and 42 fever patients. On 21 August 1847, there were 623 inmates in the workhouse and a further 181 patients in the infirmary and fever hospitals.[29] These numbers started to decline in the following weeks, which may have been due to a seasonal demand for labour, a fall in food prices, a blight-free potato crop and the Gregory clause.[30] Moreover, the Sisters of Mercy had established an industrial school for lace-making in September 1847 with a view to 'procuring employment for women and girls' in the town.[31]

Despite the decrease in demand for workhouse accommodation, there was no doubt that destitution was still prevalent in Kinsale union. Before the temporary relief ended on 29 August, there were large numbers of people receiving government-sponsored outdoor relief. On 31 July 1847, there were 8,762 persons receiving gratuitous food rations daily and a further 358 persons were buying food from the local relief committees. By 28 August the number of persons receiving gratuitous food daily had reduced to 2,638.[32] At the guardians' weekly meeting on 26 August, a cautionary note was struck by Mr Bullen, relieving officer for Ballinspittle district, who reported that the end of temporary relief would see many persons 'in utmost distress'. He added that he was authorized 'to send 100 of them into this House by provisional tickets'.[33] The decline in workhouse numbers was short-lived as once the harvest was over and the smallness of the potato crop realized, it was inevitable that the demand for poor relief would again increase.

By November 1847 the numbers seeking admission had started increasing and there was disquiet among the Carrigaline members of the board that paupers from their area were being unfairly treated under the workhouse admission policy. The guardians refuted the allegations and the majority of the board rejected a call for the formation of a separate union for the Carrigaline district. However, they acknowledged 'the necessity of extending the workhouse'.[34] This led to a committee being appointed to investigate what additional accommodation could be procured in the town. The committee consisted of the following guardians: Dr Jago, John Bird, John Heard, John Walton and Dr Daunt. During 1848 an old brewery and a disused dockyard stores were rented on a yearly basis to provide extra accommodation, in addition to the old jail that was used the previous year as an auxiliary ward of the workhouse.[35] Figure 5 shows the additional accommodation provided and the number of inmates in the workhouse.

Although there was a significant increase in auxiliary wards the standard of accommodation was extremely poor. The sheds that were hastily constructed 'were leaking and in a bad state'.[36] By March 1848, the numbers seeking admission

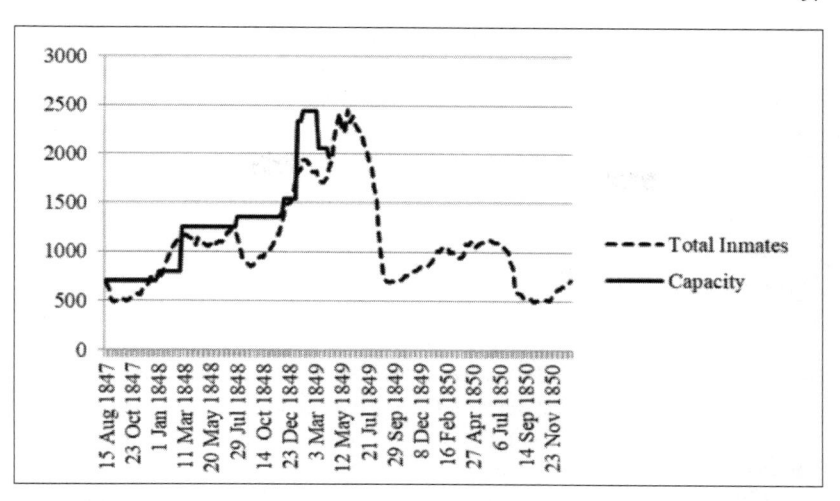

5. Total number of inmates in Kinsale workhouse (1847–51) versus capacity (1847–9)[37]

were increasing and the poor law commissioners questioned the suitability of accommodation provided for paupers at the old jail ward. In a letter to the Board they referred to the medical officer's report on the bad and unhealthy state of the ward during the previous year. The guardians acknowledged that the ward was confined in space and poorly ventilated. However, they begged the commissioners for its retention as in the event of an increase in pauperism:

> It would be able to accommodate 200 aged and infirm, hence a class not so likely to suffer from confinement, as the children who last year formed the majority of the inmates and suffered from the then prevailing epidemic.[38]

By November 1848 Kinsale union was in extreme distress after the failure of the potato crop and the poor wheat harvest. The only relief available for the destitute was the workhouse and demand for admission increased. In January 1849 there were several complaints about the bad state of the auxiliary wards and the impact the accommodation was having on the health of paupers. The commissioners were uneasy about the standard of accommodation provided and this was confirmed by reports they received. Mr Marshal, poor law inspector, presented a scathing report on the school room at the old brewery ward to the commissioners. The guardians strongly refuted the report and resolved:

> That the Commissioners be informed that the school room in question is in every respect a better one than that in which the boys school was carried on for the last two years and to which no objection was ever made by any of the Poor Law authorities, though it is not boarded neither are the school rooms in the house originally built by order of the Commissioners.

This was hardly a fair comparison as the number of boys in the workhouse had doubled over that period. On 15 January 1848 there were 216 boys under 15 years in the workhouse, whereas on 13 January 1849 there were 433 boys. Nevertheless, the guardians informed the commissioners that they were improving ventilation at the old brewery and dockyard wards so as to render them 'perfectly unobjectionable'.[39]

Another letter of complaint about the auxiliary wards was addressed to Mr Chambers, master of the workhouse, from the Roman Catholic chaplain. These complaints, and the unexplained rise in mortality from the beginning of 1849, outlined in figure 6, led the commissioners to request a return of deaths for the week ending 20 January 1849.[40] There was a grim return of 20 deaths and 14 were children under 15 years of age. On 8 February, at their weekly meeting, the guardians resolved to inform the commissioners that 500 paupers were comfortably accommodated in the old brewery the previous year and the construction of a new day room and school rooms into dormitories provided 'additional space for 300 or at least 200 more paupers'. The dockyard ward was capable of accommodating 500 boys and the fever hospital was 'calculated to accommodate 100 adults', with two additional wards under construction. On the previous Saturday there were 120 patients in the fever hospital and the guardians estimated that about 40 of them were children.[41] The guardians were satisfied with the amount and standard of accommodation they provided.

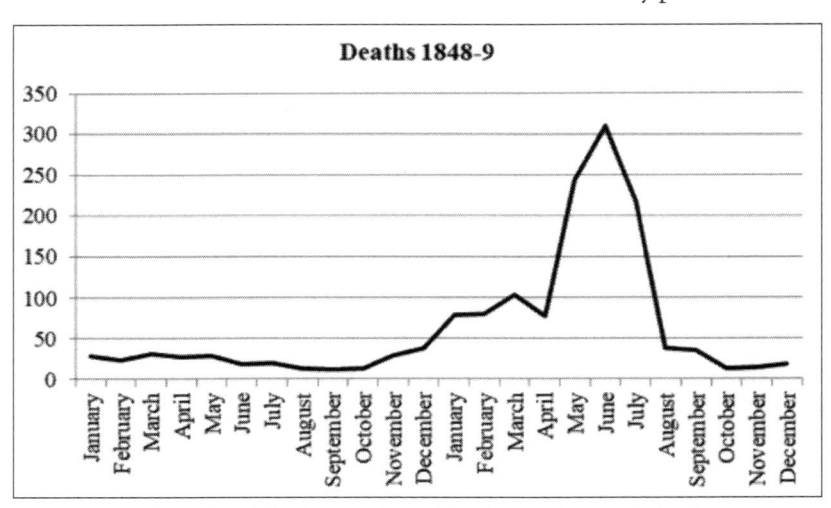

6. Number of deaths recorded in Kinsale workhouse, 1848–9[42]

During the cholera crisis additional accommodation was provided and on 26 May 1849 the number of inmates peaked at 2,455.[43] By 29 September 1849, the worst of the crisis was over and all the paupers were removed from the auxiliary wards to the workhouse. Although the crisis had peaked the suffering continued.

In January 1850, the old brewery ward was again used to accommodate inmates as the number of admissions increased. The guardians' determination to use auxiliary accommodation in preference to outdoor relief during the Famine undoubtedly added to the suffering and misery of the inmates.

WORKHOUSE STAFF

Extended accommodation inevitably brought staffing problems. The three auxiliary wards were located in the town and additional staff were required to supervise the inmates. The guardians were of the view that as the auxiliary wards were only a temporary measure the existing officers could cope with the extra duties and wards masters and mistresses could be appointed from the workhouse population. Due to the additional workload many of the officers applied for increased salaries but these were firmly rejected, with the exception of the master and the medical officer who received an additional £6 7s. and £10 respectively. The medical officer's salary increase was seen as a 'saving to the union' as he was to take on the duties of an apothecary.[44]

The workhouse population were predominantly Roman Catholic and by the end of October 1848 there was an increased workload for the Roman Catholic chaplains as they provided spiritual consolation to over 1,000 inmates.[45] A dispute arose between the guardians and Revd D. Murphy when the latter applied to the poor law commissioners for a salary increase of £15. The guardians were incensed as they objected 'to the principle that the salary of any officer of the workhouse should fluctuate with the number of paupers contained in it'. They cited the state of the union's finances, the salaries of the other officers and the grave injustice to ratepayers as mitigating circumstances.[46] The commissioners supported the salary increase in principle. On 7 December 1848, Captain Brandling attended the guardians' weekly meeting and raised the issue of the chaplain's salary. As a compromise measure Dr Jago proposed that the Board would be willing to increase the chaplain's salary to £60 per annum 'whenever a second Sunday service shall appear to the guardians to be necessary'. Immediately Revd Murphy informed the commissioners that a second Mass was necessary at the auxiliary workhouse as many were unable to attend Mass in the main workhouse. The guardians accused Revd Murphy of exaggerating the number of inmates unable to attend Mass at the workhouse and claimed he had overstated the inconvenience arising from the distance between the two wards. In order to avoid the necessity of a second Mass and unnecessary expense, the guardians resolved to remove the infirm to the main workhouse.[47] Eventually the salary of the chaplain was begrudgingly increased to £60 and remained an on-going issue until 1851. The primary consideration in the dispute was cost rather than sectarian bias on the part of the guardians, most of whom were Protestants. On 1 February 1849, they allowed the Sisters of Mercy admission to the workhouse and auxiliaries to provide religious instruction with the poor law commissioners' approval and at no expense to the union.[48]

EDUCATION

Between mid-August 1847 and the end of December 1850, women and children represented the majority of the workhouse population in Kinsale. The workhouse children were one of the most vulnerable categories and as a consequence suffered great deprivations. Children's education was just one of the areas that suffered during the Famine years. Although the poor law commissioners were firmly committed to the education and training of workhouse children the practicality of providing any standard of education became difficult if not impossible in a workhouse environment. The commissioners of national education, appointed around 1831, had oversight for the provision of a national system of elementary education in workhouse schools and offered their assistance to the boards of guardians.[49]

Kinsale board of guardians accepted the offer and on 27 January 1842 they resolved that the following school items be used in the workhouse school:

1 dozen national spelling books	1 dozen slates
1 dozen national reading books	6 dozen slate pencils
1 dozen small tables' books	6 dozen copy books

Roman Catholic and Protestant religious books were ordered for paupers of both denominations.[50] In 1844, Edward Gulson, poor law commissioner, visited Kinsale and noted that the children in Kinsale workhouse were 'making satisfactory progress'.[51] However, during the Famine years the situation changed drastically and in December 1848 and again in June 1850 the inspector of schools presented damning reports on the state of the workhouse school.

Between 1847 and 1850 the number of children in the workhouse had more than doubled and children were constantly being moved between the main workhouse and auxiliary wards. This necessitated a second school room and additional teachers. The inspector's reports highlighted the lack of school books and teaching materials, the inadequacy of the school room at the old brewery ward and the gross negligence and incompetence of the teachers.

In September 1848 the schoolmaster was dismissed on charges of immorality and many cases of insubordination and dereliction of duty were reported by the workhouse master, leaving the children unattended and uneducated.[52] The appointment of teaching staff proved very difficult for the guardians, with numerous appointments and re-appointments of the same people to different positions. In September 1848, John Carey was appointed school master on

Kinsale workhouse 61

a yearly salary of £12 and subsequently held the posts of wards master and assistant schoolmaster.⁵³ In December, John Ahern was appointed schoolmaster on a yearly salary of £15. He proved incapable of providing an acceptable standard of education to the children and Captain Brandling, poor law inspector, reported his incompetence in March 1849. Ahern was subsequently appointed ward master.⁵⁴ After placing advertisements in the Cork newspapers in March 1849, two more teachers were recruited, Mr Hyde on a salary of £21 per annum and in May, Mr Connelly. Both were dismissed after one month's trial and Ahern was reappointed schoolmaster in June 1849, despite his incompetence. By July 1849, the guardians' expressed their frustration for failing to procure a competent schoolmaster and decided to re-appoint Carey to the position as he had proved himself trustworthy and had 'gained experience'.⁵⁵

The girls' education fared little better than the boys as schoolmistresses for the workhouse school were drawn from within the workhouse population and were totally unqualified for the job. The remuneration for the post of schoolmistress was 2s. 6d. a week with rations and the appointment also involved the duties of wards mistress at the auxiliary wards. In June 1850, the guardians adopted the recommendations of the school inspector and eventually appointed a matron to the old brewery ward.⁵⁶ The low standard of education was the result of the chaos and disorder in the workhouse.

ORPHAN EMIGRATION

In 1848, the government introduced a scheme to provide female orphan emigration in conjunction with the colonial authorities in Australia. The emigration commission required suitable female candidates with a degree of education, and some moral and religious training, who could contribute to Australian society. As a high proportion of the workhouse population were female orphans, assisted emigration was welcomed by the poor law commissioners and many poor law unions.⁵⁷

Once the scheme was announced in April 1848, Kinsale board of guardians 'gladly' availed of the offer and were willing to adhere to the criteria outlined by the emigration commission for the selection of eligible, well-trained females between the ages of 14 and 18 years. A nominal list of orphans who were willing to emigrate was prepared by the master and furnished to the poor law commissioners. A list of 31 females was submitted to Major Stuart, temporary poor law inspector for Dunmanway who examined the orphans selected. On 18 May 1848, a full attendance of guardians was recorded at the board meeting where they pledged to allocate a sufficient portion of the poor rate to cover the expenses associated with the scheme. The guardians were so enthusiastic about the benefits of the scheme that they resolved to forward a second list to the poor law commissioner, 'to enable us to send out to Australia an additional number to the 31 already selected'. They viewed the scheme as an expedient way of ridding the workhouse of orphans as 'we have a great many more in this class anxious to emigrate'.[58] Moreover, the cost to the unions was minimal at around £5 per person, as the majority of the expense was borne by the colonial authorities.[59] The guardians committed to providing the necessary outfits of clothing for the girls and to pay for their transportation to Plymouth – the embarkation port for Australia. Almost a year later, Lieutenant Henry, an agent for the emigration commission, arrived in Kinsale to make the final selection of females.[60] On 16 August 1849, 29 orphans left Kinsale workhouse for Australia and the cost of their conveyance to Plymouth was £40.[61] Kinsale union was not afforded the opportunity of further reducing the number of orphans in the workhouse as the scheme ended in 1850.

EMPLOYMENT

Once the poor law was amended in 1847 the provision of work for the able-bodied was a high priority for Kinsale guardians. In the winter of 1847–8, the guardians sought the commissioners' approval for the men to collect materials for the repair of roads and for the loan of 12 pick axes, six crowbars, 20 wheelbarrows, 20 hand-barrows and 50 stone hammers from the Board of Works. Joseph Bolster was appointed steward over the men and received 6s. a week and house rations.[62]

Agricultural work was also proposed by the guardians to enable the Board to keep the paupers employed and they rented 7½ acres adjoining the workhouse from Mr Webb for this purpose. In March 1848, a horse and plough was used to prepare the field for setting potatoes. Daniel Connor was appointed superintendent for the agricultural men and on wet days he was told to make himself useful indoors. In July 1848, the guardians proposed to acquire additional land for agricultural purposes and the commissioners agreed that twenty-five acres of land could be rented.[63]

During the late 1840s many unions were attempting to establish industrial departments.[64] At their weekly meeting on 18 October 1849, there was general agreement among the Kinsale board of guardians that the workhouse should be made self-supporting. In early 1850, Kinsale workhouse began to manufacture flax and wool. A loom for weaving was already in operation and the additional activities would provide employment for the large number of able-bodied females and produce goods for the workhouse. The insurance agent was notified that flax was to be manufactured in a timber shed and the insurers of the workhouse became concerned about the dangers of the process. However, the guardians assured them that flax was to be pounded, cloved, hackled, spun and woven in a shed in the women's yard without fire or heat and the only light provided for this activity was daylight.[65] The guardians' main concern was the cost of the insurance premium rather than the working conditions for the women.

On 1 July 1852, there were 221 persons employed out of a workhouse population of 845. The men were employed in general agricultural work that produced flax, oats, potatoes and vegetables. The women were employed in tailoring, shoemaking, weaving, spinning, carding flax, wool and cotton, and domestic duties.[66] All the articles produced were used in the workhouse in a bid to reduce costs and become self-sufficient. Although the type of work had changed for the able-bodied paupers the principle remained the same – the workhouse was a place of last resort for the destitute.

During the Famine years, Kinsale workhouse struggled to cope with the crisis. The union was financially constrained, and as the crisis deepened the burden of relief meant that the guardians' attention was focused on cost-saving and financial matters. The dietary changes implemented after the loss of the potato motivated the guardians to reduce the cost of a pauper in the workhouse to a subsistence level in a bid to save money. In early 1847, overcrowding spread contagion and resulted in increased mortality, and in 1849, pestilence and disease in the workhouse caused further suffering and a high death rate. Once the full burden of relief fell on the union, the provision of three auxiliary wards at different locations around the town caused disruption to inmates' lives and staffing problems. Many of the officers were incompetent and unqualified for their roles and this resulted in the care of the most vulnerable being neglected, particularly the young and the old. One of the main priorities for the guardians was the provision of work for the able-bodied and the type of employment provided for the inmates was punitive, demoralizing and demeaning, which reflected the harshness of the system. The inadequacy of Kinsale workhouse to meet the challenges of severe distress was reflected in the high death toll, with over 2,500 deaths recorded during the Great Famine.

Conclusion

The Famine in Kinsale was a period of great human suffering. The destruction of the potato crop by the fungus *Phytophthora infestans* was an unforeseen event that caused devastation for the poorer classes who were totally dependent on it for subsistence. The failure of the poor law and the inadequacy of the various government measures to deal with extraordinary distress precipitated a chain of social dislocation, emigration, disease and death.

In the pre-Famine era, despite the improvement in the economy, more than half the people in the town of Kinsale and the majority in the rural districts lived in poverty. Kinsale workhouse, set up under the 1838 poor law to administer relief, was only availed of by the most destitute due to the harshness of the system.

With the arrival of the potato blight in 1845, the initial response by the government, although slow, was effective. The importation of food, the establishment of food depots and the provision of public works alleviated distress. The impact on Kinsale would have been almost negligible if the second crop failure had not occurred in 1846.

The consequences of the second crop failure not only affected the agricultural labourers, cottiers and small farmers but extended to other classes. The fishermen suffered as the demand for fish decreased due to the lack of a wage economy. For many, fishing was a part-time and seasonal activity and most depended on a barter system, exchanging fish for potatoes. High unemployment among the boatmen and artisans of all trades resulted as their services were no longer required or could be afforded. As the economic systems began to break down and destitution increased, distress riots resulted, but no serious disturbances were recorded in the town. In early 1847, conditions in Kinsale had become desperate and deaths from starvation were beginning to occur. The introduction of government-sponsored soup kitchens, and the role of the religious and charitable organizations in providing food to the destitute undoubtedly saved lives. The town benefited more than the rural areas from a good network of charitable organizations.

Kinsale workhouse played a subsidiary role to government relief measures during the first two years of distress. Even before the burden of famine relief fell exclusively on the union, the workhouse proved inadequate to meet the demands made on it. In early 1847, overcrowding caused the closure of the workhouse to many applicants. After August 1847, the guardians were financially constrained by the impoverished state of the union to meet the crisis. They failed to afford outdoor relief and applied the strict conditions of the workhouse test throughout the entire Famine period, which caused great hardship and suffering. A core group of guardians who regularly attended meetings appeared to have been hard working and diligent in endeavouring to address issues. There were constant problems in the workhouse with poorly constructed or rented sub-standard accommodation, poorly trained and incompetent staff, and the paupers' dietary suffered from cost-cutting measures. There was no evidence of sectarian tensions in the workhouse with the involvement of the Sisters of Mercy in religious instruction and later in medical assistance during the cholera crisis. There were clear problems in the provision of relief for children – a low level of education, disruption caused by the constant movement between auxiliary wards, and their suffering exacerbated by confinement in a fever-ridden ward.

Research shows that relapsing fever was endemic among the lower classes in Kinsale and typhus was more common among the upper classes. Fever, dysentery and other famine related diseases ebbed and flowed throughout the Famine. Deaths in the workhouse contributed to around one-fifth of the total population decrease in Kinsale union and a large number of deaths were recorded when disease was prevalent. During the first six months of 1847 and the summer of 1849, fever and cholera respectively spread contagion in the workhouse. These periods correlate to high occupancy and overcrowded conditions, which resulted in deaths.

The famine in Kinsale continued unabated until the early 1850s. The third potato crop failure and the poor wheat harvest of 1848, the cholera crisis of 1849 and the financial difficulties of the union made the scale and severity of the Great Famine in Kinsale a tragedy. The people who endured the greatest suffering were drawn from the most vulnerable classes in society. James S. Donnelly Jr asserts that pre-Famine poverty was 'very much a matter of class and famine mortality would be too'.[1] Unfortunately, this assertion held true for the people of Kinsale.

Appendices

APPENDIX I: STATISTICAL DATA FOR PATIENTS OF KINSALE FEVER HOSPITAL, JULY 1849 TO JULY 1850

Years 1849–50	Admissions	Females	Males	Paupers	Length of stay (days)	15 years of age or less
July	30	13	17	28		19
July/Aug.	30	16	14	24		15
Aug.	30	13	17	23	19	17
Sept.	30	16	14	21	24	15
Sept.	30	14	16	17	20	12
Sept./Oct.	30	20	10	18	23	13
Oct./Nov.	30	21	9	12	36	10
Jan./Feb.	30	17	13	18	26	15
Feb.	30	17	13	27	31	7
Feb.	30	16	14	24	28	9
Mar.	30	20	10	20	25	9
Mar.	30	14	16	24	28	7
Mar./Apr.	31	16	15	17	29	12
Apr.	30	12	18	23	23	13
Apr./May	30	16	14	21	26	11
May	31	20	11	20	26	9
May/June	31	16	15	23	21	8
June/July	31	16	15	24	24	14

Missing data from 17 November 1849 to 25 January 1850, reference BG108, vol. HE1.

APPENDIX 2: NUMBER OF INMATES IN KINSALE WORKHOUSE FROM 15 AUGUST 1847 TO 11 JANUARY 1851

Date	Total Inmates	Date	Total Inmates
15 Aug. 1847	679	11 Mar. 1848	1,167
21 Aug. 1847	623	18 Mar. 1848	1,155
28 Aug. 1847	503	25 Mar. 1848	1,136
4 Sept. 1847	487	1 Apr. 1848	1,128
11 Sept. 1847	495	8 Apr. 1848	1,069
18 Sept. 1847	515	15 Apr. 1848	1,135
25 Sept. 1847	532	22 Apr. 1848	1,088
2 Oct. 1847	506	29 Apr. 1848	1,087
9 Oct. 1847	492	6 May 1848	1,068
16 Oct. 1847	522	13 May 1848	1,054
23 Oct. 1847	541	20 May 1848	1,079
30 Oct. 1847	544	27 May 1848	1,042
6 Nov. 1847	566	3 June 1848	1,081
13 Nov. 1847	560	10 June 1848	1,104
20 Nov. 1847	615	17 June 1848	1,101
27 Nov. 1847	647	24 June 1848	1,130
4 Dec. 1847	663	1 July 1848	1,189
11 Dec. 1847	729	8 July 1848	1,212
18 Dec. 1847	732	15 July 1848	1,241
25 Dec. 1847	742	22 July 1848	1,196
1 Jan. 1848	757	29 July 1848	1,159
8 Jan. 1848	757	5 Aug. 1848	1,029
15 Jan. 1848	830	12 Aug. 1848	944
22 Jan. 1848	903	19 Aug. 1848	890
29 Jan. 1848	976	26 Aug. 1848	874
5 Feb. 1848	1,030	2 Sept. 1848	846
12 Feb. 1848	1,080	9 Sept. 1848	862
19 Feb. 1848	1,104	16 Sept. 1848	897
26 Feb. 1848	1,132	30 Sept. 1848	928
4 Mar. 1848	1,148	7 Oct. 1848	955

APPENDIX 2: NUMBER OF INMATES IN KINSALE WORKHOUSE FROM 15 AUGUST 1847 TO 11 JANUARY 1851 *(continued)*

Date	Total Inmates	Date	Total Inmates
14 Oct. 1848	944	12 May 1849	2,227
21 Oct. 1848	1,005	19 May 1849	2,233
28 Oct. 1848	1,004	26 May 1849	2,455
4 Nov. 1848	1,041	2 June 1849	2,327
11 Nov. 1848	1,090	9 June 1849	2,384
18 Nov. 1848	1,143	16 June 1849	2,306
25 Nov. 1848	1,191	23 June 1849	2,240
2 Dec. 1848	1,296	30 June 1849	2,234
9 Dec. 1848	1,405	7 July 1849	2,117
16 Dec. 1848	1,484	14 July 1849	2,033
23 Dec. 1848	1,499	21 July 1849	1,938
30 Dec. 1848	1,546	28 July 1849	1,862
6 Jan. 1849	1,732	4 Aug. 1849	1,665
13 Jan. 1849	1,813	11 Aug. 1849	1,533
20 Jan. 1849	1,837	18 Aug. 1849	1,185
27 Jan. 1849	1,933	25 Aug. 1849	892
3 Feb. 1849	1,930	1 Sept. 1849	723
10 Feb. 1849	1,909	8 Sept. 1849	699
17 Feb. 1849	1,819	15 Sept. 1849	692
24 Feb. 1849	1,806	22 Sept. 1849	698
3 Mar. 1849	1,822	29 Sept. 1849	697
10 Mar. 1849	1,733	6 Oct. 1849	705
17 Mar. 1849	1,703	13 Oct. 1849	717
24 Mar. 1849	1,710	20 Oct. 1849	725
31 Mar. 1849	1,759	27 Oct. 1849	754
7 Apr. 1849	1,856	3 Nov. 1849	766
14 Apr. 1849	1,959	10 Nov. 1849	775
21 Apr. 1849	2,169	17 Nov. 1849	802
28 Apr. 1849	2,325	24 Nov. 1849	803
5 May 1849	2,419	1 Dec. 1849	830

APPENDIX 2: NUMBER OF INMATES IN KINSALE WORKHOUSE FROM 15 AUGUST 1847 TO 11 JANUARY 1851 (continued)

Date	Total Inmates	Date	Total Inmates
8 Dec. 1849	843	6 July 1850	1,078
15 Dec. 1849	863	13 July 1850	1,064
22 Dec. 1849	851	20 July 1850	1,029
29 Dec. 1849	873	27 July 1850	998
5 Jan. 1850	897	3 Aug. 1850	910
12 Jan. 1850	956	10 Aug. 1850	839
19 Jan. 1850	1,010	17 Aug. 1850	610
26 Jan. 1850	999	24 Aug. 1850	579
2 Feb. 1850	1,047	31 Aug. 1850	577
9 Feb. 1850	1,050	7 Sept. 1850	535
16 Feb. 1850	1,052	14 Sept. 1850	521
23 Feb. 1850	996	21 Sept. 1850	531
2 Mar. 1850	1,000	28 Sept. 1850	524
9 Mar. 1850	969	5 Oct. 1850	497
16 Mar. 1850	943	12 Oct. 1850	504
23 Mar. 1850	937	19 Oct. 1850	510
30 Mar. 1850	958	26 Oct. 1850	510
6 Apr. 1850	1,085	2 Nov. 1850	518
13 Apr. 1850	1,078	9 Nov. 1850	518
20 Apr. 1850	1,102	16 Nov. 1850	511
27 Apr. 1850	1,103	23 Nov. 1850	544
4 May 1850	1,056	30 Nov. 1850	592
11 May 1850	1,083	7 Dec. 1850	623
18 May 1850	1,096	14 Dec. 1850	632
25 May 1850	1,110	21 Dec. 1850	649
1 June 1850	1,127	28 Dec. 1850	648
8 June 1850	1,123	4 Jan. 1851	678
15 June 1850	1,113	11 Jan. 1851	716
22 June 1850	1,101		
29 June 1850	1,094		

Notes

ABBREVIATIONS

BG108/A   Kinsale Board of Guardians Minute books
BG108/G   Kinsale Board of Guardians Indoor Relief Registers
BG108/HE   Kinsale Board of Guardians Register of Patients of Fever Hospital
BG108/KA   Kinsale Board of Guardians Record of Deaths book
CCCA   Cork City and County Archives
HC   House of Commons
NAI   National Archives of Ireland
RLFC   Relief commission papers

I. PRE-FAMINE KINSALE

1 James S. Donnelly Jr, *The great Irish potato famine* (Stroud, 2001), p. 1.
2 Virginia Crossman, *The poor law in Ireland, 1838–1948* (Dublin, 2006), p. 7.
3 Christine Kinealy, *This great calamity: the Irish famine, 1845–52* (Dublin, 2006), pp 10–11.
4 *The parliamentary gazetteer of Ireland* (London, 1846), II, p. 566.
5 Samuel Lewis, *A topographical dictionary of Ireland* (London, 1837), II, pp 232–3.
6 *Parliamentary gazetteer*, p. 568.
7 Lewis, *A topographical dictionary of Ireland*, p. 232.
8 *Parliamentary gazetteer*, p. 568.
9 Donal O'Leary and Vincent Murphy, 'Milling in the Kinsale area', *Journal of the Kinsale & District Local History Society*, 13 (2005), 45.
10 *Parliamentary gazetteer*, p. 568.
11 Lewis, *A topographical dictionary of Ireland*, p. 232.
12 R.B. McDowell, 'Ireland on the eve of the Famine' in R. Dudley Edwards and T. Desmond Williams (eds), *The Great Famine: studies in Irish history, 1845–52* (Dublin, 1956), p. 3.
13 Donnelly, *The great Irish potato famine*, pp 3–4.
14 Leslie J. Dowley, 'The potato and late blight in Ireland' in Cormac Ó Gráda (ed), *Famine 150: Commemorative lecture series* (Dublin, 1997), p. 56.
15 *Population, Ireland, census of the population, 1831: Comparative abstract of the population in Ireland, as taken in 1821 and 1831*, HC 1833 [23], xxxix, p. 23.
16 *Report of the commissioners appointed to take the census of Ireland for the year 1841*, HC 1843 [504], xxiv, p. 186 (henceforth cited as *Census Ire.*, 1841).
17 Ibid., pp 186–7.
18 *Parliamentary gazetteer*, p. 566.
19 Convent of Mercy, Kinsale, annals, vol. 2, (unpublished).
20 Donnelly, *The great Irish potato famine*, p. 2.
21 *Census Ire.*, 1841, pp 186–7.
22 Patrick Hickey, *Famine in West Cork: the Mizen Peninsula, land and people, 1800–1852: a local study of pre-Famine and Famine Ireland* (Cork, 2002), pp 135–6.
23 Kinealy, *This great calamity*, pp 18–19.
24 *First report from His Majesty's commissioners for inquiring into the condition of the poorer classes in Ireland, with appendix and supplement*, HC 1835 [369], xxxii, p. 673 (henceforth cited as *Poor Inquiry*).
25 Laurence M. Geary, '"The whole country was in motion": mendicancy and vagrancy in pre-Famine Ireland' in Jacqueline R. Hill and Colm Lennon (eds), *Luxury and austerity. Historical Studies xxi* (Dublin, 1999), p. 121.
26 *Poor Inquiry*, pp 673–4.
27 Ibid.
28 Dympna McLoughlin, 'The impact of the Great Famine on subsistent women' in John Crowley, William J. Smyth and

Michael Murphy (eds), *Atlas of the Great Irish Famine* (Cork, 2012), p. 255.
29 *Poor Inquiry*, p. 161.
30 Lewis, *A topographical dictionary of Ireland*, p. 233.
31 *Poor Inquiry*, pp 252–3.
32 Laurence M. Geary, *Medicine and charity in Ireland, 1718–1851* (Dublin, 2004), p. 2.
33 *Parliamentary gazetteer*, p. 568.
34 *Poor Inquiry*, pp 327–9.
35 Ibid., pp 327–8.
36 Ibid., p. 444.
37 Ibid.
38 Ibid., p. 443.
39 Ibid.
40 *Evidence taken before Her Majesty's commissioners of inquiry into the state of the law and practice in respect to the occupation of land in Ireland*, Part II, HC 1845 [616], xx, p. 988 (henceforth cited as *Inquiry into the occupation of land in Ireland*).
41 Ibid., p. 994.
42 James S. Donnelly Jr, *The land and the people of nineteenth-century Cork: the rural economy and the land question* (London, 1975), p. 29.
43 *Inquiry into the occupation of land in Ireland*, pp 986–9.
44 Ibid., pp 985–96.
45 Donnelly, *The great Irish potato famine*, p. 2.
46 Crossman, *The poor law in Ireland*, pp 8–11.
47 *Parliamentary gazetteer*, p. 568.
48 CCCA, BG108, vol. G1, Kinsale Indoor Relief Register, p. 2.
49 CCCA, BG108, vol. A1, Kinsale Board of Guardian Minute book, pp 29–31.
50 CCCA, BG108, vol. G1, pp 4–96. The number 1765 reflects the number in the Indoor Relief Register book and as pages 14–15 are missing (16 June–14 July 1842) these admissions are omitted from the total number and resulting computations.
51 Ibid., pp 5–89.
52 Kinealy, *This great calamity*, p. 25.
53 William J. Smyth, 'The roles of cities and towns during the Great Famine' in Crowley, Smyth, and Murphy (eds), *Atlas of the Great Irish Famine*, p. 241.

2. FAMINE, DEATH AND DISEASE IN KINSALE UNION

1 Cormac Ó Gráda and Andrés Eiríksson (eds), *Ireland's Great Famine: interdisciplinary perspectives* (Dublin, 2006), p. 7.
2 Donnelly, *The land and the people of Cork*, p. 73.
3 Kinealy, *This great calamity*, p. 38.
4 John Feehan, 'The potato: root of the Famine' in Crowley, Smyth and Murphy (eds), *Atlas of the Great Irish Famine*, p. 33.
5 Laurence M. Geary, 'The Great Famine in County Cork: a socio-medical analysis' in Michael Willem De Nie and Sean Farrell (eds), *Power and popular culture in modern Ireland: essays in honour of James S. Donnelly Jr* (Dublin, 2010), p. 31.
6 Dowley, 'The potato and late blight in Ireland', p. 56.
7 Donnelly, *The great Irish potato famine*, pp 41–2.
8 *Kerry Evening Post*, 17 Sept. 1845.
9 Donnelly, *The great Irish potato famine*, p. 43.
10 *Kerry Evening Post*, 17 Sept. 1845.
11 Ciarán Ó Murchadha, *The Great Famine: Ireland's agony, 1845–1852* (London, 2011), p. 29.
12 Feehan, 'The potato: root of the Famine', p. 30.
13 Constabulary report to relief commissioners, 29 Oct. 1845 (NAI, RLFC, 2/Z/14920).
14 CCCA, BG108, vol. A2, pp 253–4; see also letter from Kinsale board of guardians to Lord Bandon, 28 Nov. 1845 (NAI, RLFC, 2/Z/16848).
15 Donnelly, *The great Irish potato famine*, pp 44–5.
16 Kinealy, *This great calamity*, pp 38, 46, 61.
17 CCCA, BG108, vol. A2, pp 241, 247, 256; note that the subsequent minute book, BG108, vol. A3, covering a period from 2 April 1846 to 26 August 1847, is missing from the archives.
18 Kinealy, *This great calamity*, p. 66.
19 CCCA, BG108, vol. A2, p. 261.
20 Constabulary report to relief commissioners, 17 Dec. 1845 (NAI, RLFC, 1/41).
21 Coastguard report to relief commissioners, 15 Jan. 1846 (NAI, RLFC, 3/1/366).

22 Laurence M. Geary, 'What people died of during the Famine' in Ó Gráda (ed.), *Famine 150*, p. 96.
23 CCCA, BG108, vol. A2, pp 307–8.
24 Ibid., pp 221, 312.
25 Ibid., pp 298–9.
26 J. Hosford, clerk of Kinsale poor law union to relief commissioners, 19 Apr. 1846 (NAI, RLFC, 3/1/1396).
27 Relief commissioners to J. Hosford, 13 Apr. 1846 (NAI, RLFC, 3/1/1424).
28 CCCA, BG108, vol. A2, p. 303.
29 Revd J.B. Webb to relief commissioners, 26 Mar. 1846, (NAI, RLFC, 3/1/1047).
30 *Scarcity Commission: Further return showing the progress of disease in the potatoes, the complaints which have been made, and the applications for relief, for the week ending the 4th day of April 1846*, HC 1846 [213], xxxvii, p. 3.
31 *Cork Examiner*, 19 Nov. 1845.
32 Kinealy, *This great calamity*, p. 44.
33 *Correspondence explanatory of the measures adopted by Her Majesty's government for the relief of distress arising from the failure of the potato crop in Ireland*, HC 1846 [735], xxxvii, pp 218–19 (henceforth cited as *Correspondence explanatory of measures adopted*, 1846).
34 Thomas P. O'Neill, 'The organization and administration of relief' in Edwards and Williams (eds), *The Great Famine*, p. 213.
35 Kinealy, *This great calamity*, pp 48–9.
36 *Correspondence explanatory of measures adopted*, 1846, p. 218.
37 'From *Southern Reporter*' in *Freeman's Journal*, 4 Apr. 1846.
38 Kinealy, *This great calamity*, p. 41.
39 *Cork Examiner*, 22 Apr. 1846.
40 *Correspondence explanatory of measures adopted*, 1846, p. 16.
41 John Heard, chairman of Kinsale relief committee to relief commissioners, 10 Apr. 1846 (NAI, RFLC, 3/1/1393).
42 Kinealy, *This great calamity*, pp 44–5.
43 O'Neill, 'The organization and administration of relief', p. 217.
44 *Correspondence explanatory of measures adopted*, 1846, pp 236–9.
45 Donnelly, *The great Irish potato famine*, p. 49.
46 Thomas Cuthbert, Ballinspittle relief committee to relief commissioners, 27 May 1846 (NAI, RLFC, 3/1/2641).

47 *Cork Examiner*, 15 May 1846.
48 *Correspondence explanatory of measures adopted*, 1846, pp 162–3.
49 *Cork Examiner*, 15 May 1846.
50 Kinealy, *This great calamity*, p. 54.
51 *Correspondence explanatory of measures adopted*, 1846, pp 316, 325, 338, 369, 372.
52 Ibid., p. 318.
53 Innishannon relief committee to relief commissioners, 11 May 1846 (NAI, RLFC, 3/1/2186).
54 Relief commissioners to Innishannon relief committee, 22 June 1846 (NAI, RLFC, 3/1/3536).
55 *Cork Examiner*, 27 May 1846.
56 Donnelly, *The great Irish potato famine*, p. 55.
57 *Correspondence explanatory of measures adopted*, 1846, p. 314.
58 *Cork Examiner*, 17 June 1846.
59 Ibid., 15 May 1846.
60 Kinealy, *This great calamity*, pp 71–2.
61 *Cork Examiner*, 14 Aug. 1846.
62 'From *Cork Constitution*' in *Kerry Evening Post*, 15 Aug. 1846.
63 *Cork Examiner*, 10 Aug. 1846.
64 Donnelly, *The land and the people of Cork*, p. 74.
65 *Cork Examiner*, 14 Aug. 1846.
66 J. Heard, chairman of Kinsale relief committee to relief commissioners, 20 Aug. 1846 (NAI, RLFC, 3/1/5499).
67 Donnelly, *The land and the people of Cork*, p. 84.
68 O'Neill, 'The organization and administration of relief', p. 223.
69 Kinealy, *This great calamity*, p. 90.
70 O'Neill, 'The organization and administration of relief', p. 228.
71 *Cork Examiner*, 4 Sept. 1846.
72 *Freeman's Journal*, 14 Sept. 1846.
73 Donnelly, *The great Irish potato famine*, p. 60.
74 *Cork Examiner*, 28 Sept. 1846.
75 O'Neill, 'The organization and administration of relief', p. 228.
76 *Cork Examiner*, 7 Oct. 1846.
77 *Reproductive works (Kinsale). Copies of correspondence on the subject of certain reproductive works presented at the sessions held for the barony of Kinsale, on the 5th day of October last, under the Labour Rate*, HC 1847 [182], lvi, pp 1–2 (henceforth cited as *Reproductive works (Kinsale)*, 1847).

Notes

78 Kinealy, *This great calamity*, p. 90.
79 *Cork Examiner*, 7 Oct. 1846.
80 Kinealy, *This great calamity*, p. 90.
81 *Reproductive works (Kinsale)*, 1847, pp 6–9.
82 Kinealy, *This great calamity*, p. 92.
83 Donnelly, *The great Irish potato famine*, pp 72–3.
84 'From *Southern Reporter*' in *Freeman's Journal*, 6 Nov. 1846.
85 Hickey, *Famine in West Cork*, p. 157.
86 *Cork Examiner*, 23 Nov. 1846.
87 Ibid., 14 Dec. 1846.
88 Kinealy, *This great calamity*, p. 93.
89 *Cork Examiner*, 14 Dec. 1846.
90 Donnelly, *The land and the people of Cork*, p. 72.
91 Kinealy, *This great calamity*, p. 92.
92 *Cork Examiner*, 14 Dec. 1846.
93 O'Neill, 'The organization and administration of relief ', p. 231.
94 *Freeman's Journal*, 5 Dec. 1846.
95 Kinealy, *This great calamity*, pp 79, 89.
96 *Cork Examiner*, 22 Feb. 1847.
97 Ibid.
98 Ibid.
99 Ibid.
100 Ibid.
101 *Reproductive works (Kinsale)*, 1847, p. 10.
102 Hickey, *Famine in West Cork*, p. 167.
103 Convent of Mercy, Kinsale, annals, vol. 2.
104 Christine Kinealy, *Charity and the great hunger in Ireland: the kindness of strangers* (London, 2013), p. 154.
105 Central Relief Committee of the Society of Friends, *Transactions of the central relief committee of the Society of Friends during the Famine in Ireland, in 1846 and 1847: With an index by Rob Goodbody* (Dublin, 1996), pp 174–6, (henceforth cited as *Transactions of the central relief committee of the Society of Friends*).
106 O'Neill, 'The organization and administration of relief ', p. 235.
107 *Transactions of the central relief committee of the Society of Friends*, pp 174–6.
108 Kinealy, *Charity and the great hunger*, p. 154.
109 *Transactions of the central relief committee of the Society of Friends*, pp 174–6.
110 *Cork Examiner*, 12 Feb. 1847.
111 *Census of Ireland. A comparative view of the census of Ireland in 1841 and 1851; Distinguishing the several unions and electoral divisions, and showing the area and population of those districts respectively*, HC 1852 [373], xlvi, p. 25.
112 *Report of the commissioners of health, Ireland, on the epidemics of 1846 to 1850*, HC 1852–3 [1562], xli, p. 1 (henceforth cited as *Report of the commissioners of health*).
113 L. Geary, 'Medical relief and the Great Famine' in Crowley, Smyth and Murphy (eds), *Atlas of the Great Irish Famine*, p. 199.
114 *Report of the commissioners of health*, pp 20–1.
115 *Cork Examiner*, 22 Feb. 1847.
116 Ibid., 3 Feb. 1847.
117 Ibid.
118 Ibid., 12 Feb. 1847.
119 Geary, 'The Great Famine in County Cork: a socio-medical analysis', p. 35.
120 *Cork Examiner*, 1 Feb. 1847.
121 William P. MacArthur, 'Medical history of the Famine' in Edwards and Williams (eds), *The Great Famine*, p. 279.
122 Geary, 'The Great Famine in County Cork: a socio-medical analysis', p. 35.
123 Geary, 'Medical relief and the Great Famine', p. 199.
124 Ó Murchadha, *The Great Famine: Ireland's agony*, p. 90.
125 *Disease (Ireland). Abstracts of the most serious representations made by the several medical superintendents of public institutions*, HC 1846 [120], xxxvii, p. 3.
126 Geary, 'Medical relief and the Great Famine', pp 199–200.
127 MacArthur, 'Medical history of the Famine', p. 292.
128 CCCA, BG108, vol. A2, pp 273, 283, 297.
129 Ibid., pp 283–4.
130 *Cork Examiner*, 18 May 1846.
131 Ibid., 14 Dec. 1846.
132 Ibid., 22 Feb. 1847.
133 *Cork Examiner*, 7 Oct. 1846.
134 CCCA, BG108, vol. A4, pp 37 and 288.
135 CCCA, BG108, vol. G1, pp 138–340.
136 MacArthur, 'Medical history of the Famine', p. 291.
137 CCCA, BG108, vol. KA1, Kinsale Record of Deaths book, data missing from 25 to 31 Mar. 1847.

138 Laurence M. Geary, *Medicine and charity in Ireland*, pp 187–91.
139 *Distress (Ireland): Third report of the relief commissioners, constituted under the Act 10th Vic., cap. 7*, HC 1847 [836], xvii, pp 12–13.
140 CCCA, BG108, vol. A4, p. 37.
141 Kinealy, *This great calamity*, p. 177.
142 CCCA, BG108, vol. A4, pp 72, 76, 100, 119, 226.
143 MacArthur, 'Medical history of the Famine', p. 276.
144 *Report of the commissioners of health*, p. 12.
145 CCCA, BG108, vol. HE1, Record of patients in fever hospital, reference appendix 1 for data.
146 *Cork Examiner*, 30 Mar. 1849.
147 CCCA, BG108, vol. KA1.
148 Geary, 'What people died of during the Famine', p. 108.
149 MacArthur, 'Medical history of the Famine', pp 306–7.
150 *Report of the commissioners of health*, pp 30 and 70.
151 CCCA, BG108, vol. A4, pp 686, 737, 838, 848, 857.
152 Kinealy, *This great calamity*, p. 253.
153 CCCA, BG108, vol. A4, pp 858, 878, 887, 888.
154 Ibid., pp 877, 888, 897.
155 *Kerry Evening Post*, 23 May 1849.
156 CCCA, BG108, vol. A4, p. 917.
157 Joseph Robins, *The Miasma: epidemic and panic in nineteenth-century Ireland* (Dublin, 1995), p. 142.
158 *Cork Examiner*, 30 May 1849.
159 CCCA, BG108, vol. A4, pp 917, 927, 937.
160 *Report of the commissioners of health*, p. 36.
161 *Cork Examiner*, 30 May 1849.

3. KINSALE WORKHOUSE

1 *First annual report of the commissioners for administering the laws for relief of the poor in Ireland, with appendices*, HC 1847–8 [963], xxxiii, p. 13.
2 Crossman, *The poor law in Ireland, 1838–1948*, p. 11.
3 John O'Connor, *The workhouses of Ireland: the fate of Ireland's poor* (Dublin, 1995), pp 80–5.
4 Michelle O'Mahony, *The Famine in Cork city: Famine life at Cork union workhouse* (Cork, 2005), p. 20.
5 Colman Mahony, *Cork's poor law palace: workhouse life, 1838–1890* (Monkstown, Co. Cork, 2005), p. xii.
6 Crossman, *The poor law in Ireland, 1838–1948*, p. 14.
7 Mahony, *Cork's poor law palace*, p. xiii.
8 Crossman, *The poor law in Ireland, 1838–1948*, p. 14.
9 Mahony, *Cork's poor law palace*, p. 1.
10 CCCA, BG108, vol. A4, vol. A5, vol. A6.
11 Desmond McCabe and Cormac Ó Gráda, '"Better off thrown behind a ditch": Enniskillen workhouse during the Great Famine' in De Nie and Farrell (eds), *Power and popular culture in modern Ireland*, p. 13.
12 Mahony, *Cork's poor law palace*, p. 21.
13 O'Connor, *The workhouses of Ireland*, p. 101.
14 CCCA, BG108, vol. A1, pp 77–8.
15 *Correspondence explanatory of measures adopted*, 1846, pp 226–30.
16 *Report of the commissioners of health*, p.58.
17 CCCA, BG108, vol. A4, p. 408.
18 CCCA, BG108, vol. A6, pp 159, 171, 183, 195.
19 Ibid., p. 304.
20 Ibid., pp 255–397.
21 CCCA, BG108, vol. A2, vol. A4, vol. A6.
22 Kinealy, *This great calamity*, p. 113.
23 Ibid., p. 180.
24 Crossman, *The poor law in Ireland, 1838–1948*, p. 24.
25 Donnelly, *The great Irish potato famine*, p. 110.
26 Crossman, *The poor law in Ireland, 1838–1948*, p. 24.
27 Kinealy, *This great calamity*, p. 181.
28 *Commissioners for administering laws for relief of poor in Ireland: second annual report with appendices*, HC 1849 [1118], xxv, p. 13.
29 CCCA, BG108, vol. A4, p. 1.
30 Donnelly, *The great Irish potato famine*, p. 102.
31 Convent of Mercy, Kinsale, annals, p. 11.
32 *Fifth, sixth, and seventh reports of the relief commissioners, constituted under the Act 10th Vic., cap. 7; and correspondence connected therewith*, HC 1847–8 [876], xxix, p. 8 (fifth report, appendix I), and p. 9 (sixth report, appendix I).

Notes

33 CCCA, BG108, vol. A4, p. 7.
34 Ibid., pp 118–19.
35 Ibid., p. 109.
36 Ibid., p. 97.
37 CCCA, BG108, vol. A4, vol. A5, vol. A6, reference Appendix 2 for inmate data.
38 CCCA, BG108, vol. A4, p. 286.
39 Ibid., pp 726–7.
40 Ibid., pp 741–8.
41 Ibid., p. 758.
42 CCCA, BG108, vol. KA1, Kinsale Record of Deaths book.
43 CCCA, BG108, vol. A4, p. 881.
44 Ibid., pp 606–7.
45 CCCA, BG108, vol. G1, vol. G2.
46 CCCA, BG108, vol. A4, pp 606–7.
47 Ibid., pp 667 and 776–7.
48 Ibid., p. 746.
49 Joseph Robins, *The lost children: a study of charity children in Ireland, 1700–1900* (Dublin, 1980), pp 222–3.
50 CCCA, BG108, vol. A1, pp 101–2.
51 Robins, *The lost children*, p. 224.
52 CCCA, BG108, vol. A4, p. 557.
53 Ibid., pp 567, 627, 687, 717, 728.
54 Ibid., pp 667, 756, 796, 897.
55 Ibid., pp 846, 878, 957, 967.
56 CCCA, BG108, vol. A6, p. 42.
57 Kinealy, *This great calamity*, pp 315–17.
58 CCCA, BG108, vol. A4, pp 327, 346 and 377–8.
59 Kinealy, *This great calamity*, pp 311–16.
60 CCCA, BG108, vol. A4, pp 327 and 856.
61 CCCA, BG108, vol. A5, pp 14, 399, 408.
62 CCCA, BG108, vol. A4, pp 217 and 237.
63 Ibid., pp 126–7, 297, 305, 317, 476.
64 Mahony, *Cork's poor law palace*, p. 145.
65 CCCA, BG108, vol. A5, pp 117 and 279.
66 *Abstract return from poor law unions in England, Wales and Ireland on employment in workhouses or land attached; number of adult able-bodied persons engaged in handicraft and agricultural industry, July 1852*, HC 1852–3 [513], lxxxiv, pp 26–7.

CONCLUSION

1 Donnelly, *The great Irish potato famine*, p. 2.